Teaching Motor Skills

Teaching Motor Skills

Bryant J. Cratty
University of California, Los Angeles

Prentice-Hall, Inc., *Englewood Cliffs, New Jersey*

Library of Congress Cataloging in Publication Data

CRATTY, BRYANT J
   Teaching motor skills.

   Includes bibliographies.
   1. Perceptual-motor learning.   I. Title.
LB1067.C75   152.3'34   72–6137
ISBN 0-13-893966-7
ISBN 0-13-893958-6 (pbk.)

© 1973 by Prentice-Hall, Inc., Englewood Cliffs, N.J.

All rights reserved. No part of this book may be reproduced in any form or by any means without permission in writing from the publisher.

Printed in the United States of America

10 9 8 7 6 5 4 3 2 1

Prentice-Hall International, Inc., *London*
Prentice-Hall of Australia, Pty. Ltd., *Sydney*
Prentice-Hall of Canada, Ltd., *Toronto*
Prentice-Hall of India Private Limited, *New Delhi*
Prentice-Hall of Japan, Inc., *Tokyo*

Figures 2.4, 2.5, 2.6, 2.7, 2.8, and 2.9 reprinted from Edwin A. Fleishman, *The Structure and Measurement of Physical Fitness*, © 1964, by permission of Prentice-Hall, Inc., Englewood Cliffs, New Jersey.

Contents

1 **INTRODUCTION**   1

    What Is a Motor Skill?   5
    Types of Motor Skills   7
    Perception and Motion   10
    What Is Teaching?   11
    Summary   12
    Discussion Questions and Exercises   13
    Bibliography   13

2 **MOTOR PERFORMANCE**   15

    Fine and Gross Motor Skills   16
    Typology Based on a Consideration of Task Complexity   18
    Simple Movements   19
    Compound Tasks   19
    Complex Movements   19
    Physical Ability Traits: Their Identification and Implications   21

vi   CONTENTS

         Reaction Time, Movement Speed, Response Time   32
         Motor Performance—An Overview   35
         Discussion Questions and Exercises   37
         Bibliography   37

3   ACQUIRING MOTOR SKILL   39

         Individual versus Group Performance Curves   43
         Learning versus Performance   47
         Skill Acquisition Over Time   48
         Motor Educability   48
         The Measurement of Motor Learning   50
         Summary   52
         Discussion Questions and Exercises   53
         Bibliography   54

4   INSTRUCTIONS   55

         Learners Talk to Themselves!   56
         Instructions in Time   57
         Sensory Channel   60
         Instructions through Vision   60
         Verbal Instructions   62
         Instructions through Movement   63
         Whose Instructions Are Important?   64
         Summary   66
         Discussion Questions and Exercises   67
         Bibliography   68

5   QUANTITATIVE, QUALITATIVE, AND TEMPORAL ASPECTS OF MOTOR SKILL PRACTICE   69

         Massing and Distributing Practice in Time   70
         The Variety of Practice Schedules   70
         Effects of Timing on Performance Levels   72
         Why Spacing Practice Sometimes Helps   74
         Whole versus Part Practice   75
         Progressive-Part Practice   75
         Whole Practice   76
         Speed versus Accuracy   77

Summary 78
Discussion Questions and Exercises 79
Bibliography 80

6 MOTIVATION AND ACTIVATION 81

Motivation 82
Movation Viewed Developmentally 82
Types of Rewards and Their Influence on Motor
Performance 82
The Complexity of the Task 83
Novelty 83
Psychological Needs and Motives 83
The Need to Struggle to Overcome Obstacles 83
The Need to Exhibit Excellence 84
The Need for Status 84
Affiliation Needs 84
Tangible Rewards 84
Social Motives and Rewards 85
Measuring Motives and Teacher Sensitivity 87
Activation 88
Adjusting the Importance of the Contest 90
Adjusting the Social Conditions 90
"Obliterating" the Contest 90
Relaxation Training (Psychotonic Training) 91
Help the Performer Understand and Accept Signs of
Activation 91
Summary 91
Discussion Questions and Exercises 92
Bibliography 93

7 INTELLIGENCE AND SKILL ACQUISITION 94

Intellectual Components of Motor Skill Learning 95
Fitness, Academic Performance, and Intelligence 98
Intellectual Demands in Athletics 99
Tactical Training 100
Memory 102
General Information 103
Discussion Questions and Exercises 104
Bibliography 105

8 TRANSFER OF SKILL — 106

The Evaluation of Transfer Effects   107
Bilateral Transfer   108
Intertask Transfer   112
Learning Sets   114
Positive and Negative Effects   115
Many Transferable Elements   116
Summary   117
Discussion Questions and Exercises   119
Bibliography   120

9 RETENTION OF MOTOR SKILL — 121

Theories of Retention   123
The Measurement of Retention   126
Short-Term Retention of Motor Skills   126
Long-Term Retention of Discrete Responses   128
An Overview   129
Aiding Retention of Skill   129
Summary   132
Discussion Questions and Exercises   133
Bibliography   133

10 SUMMARY AND OVERVIEW — 135

Variety in Teaching Methods   136
Give Learners Time   136
Be Cautious of Overteaching   137
Involve the Learner Intellectually   137
Transmit Reasons and Meanings of Movement   137
Emotional Aura Is Important   138
Make Drills Effective   138
Quick Improvement Is Motivating   139
Retention Is Best When Skills Are Well Learned   139
Conclusion   139

INDEX   141

Preface

Teaching motor skills is a principal American vocation and avocation. As soon as an individual even superficially acquires a new sport, he becomes an instant expert and sets out forthwith to teach others. I have often been amused at the sight of a youth on a trampoline, attempting to respond to the directions of "coaches" on all sides.

Despite the high interest in the teaching of skills, however, they are often not well taught. They are sometimes over-taught, that is, the performer is bombarded with too much information from too many sources. Or instructions may not be paced correctly or may be "pitched" at a level too high or low for the performer. At other times, the emotional environment created by the instructor or coach is so stressful that it defeats his best attempts to inform the learner about the essentials of the skill to be mastered.

This book is a collection of reasonably sound guidelines for teaching motor skills. It should prove useful to coaches attempting to teach youths the fundamentals of Little League sports, to school athletic coaches and physical education teachers, to instructors in dental schools, to foremen trying to maximize the skills of factory workers, to preschool teachers of school readiness skills such as eye–hand coordination needed for rudimentary printing, and to people in many other situations involving motor skills.

I would like to express my appreciation to the editors at Prentice-Hall, including Walter Welch and Carolyn Davidson, for their help in producing the manuscript. My office staff, Margie Hamano, Donna Hokoda, and Brian Tash, also helped in the execution of the final manuscript. I hope that my efforts and theirs have produced a guide that will help those attempting to improve skilled performance in a variety of contexts.

Teaching Motor Skills

I

Introduction

Within the past century, careful observations by naturalists have revealed what are apparently formal attempts on the part of animals to teach their offspring skills essential to survival. Such tutorial behavior, which seems too complex to label simply "instinctual," ranges from the efforts of the lioness to impart hunting skills to her young to the teaching of gymnastic stunts by the mothers of some of the larger and more advanced primate species.

It is not surprising, therefore, to find a great deal of evidence that primitive hominids showed marked concern in teaching skills necessary for making simple tools, for hunting, and for dealing in other ways with the often hostile environment. Present-day counterparts to those primitive efforts are found in the Australian aborigine and the African bushman. The adult members of these remnants of prehistorical human cultures take great pains to transmit to their children the essential stalking and trapping skills needed to ensnare small game. Tool making is similarly taught by members of these contemporary tribes.

From prehistory, progressive societies have paid varying amounts of attention to the acquisition of physical skills. Much of the time, skills which might be classified as "motor," involving accurate movement of the larger muscles, were taught in both formal and informal ways. Fathers casually taught their sons the essential farm tasks, while more structured organizations were established at various times in history to transmit the skills of knighthood, handwriting, silver working, and so on. In the nineteenth century several parallel but at first unrelated threads gradually coalesced to engender interest in the scientific exploration of how man learns and teaches complex movement skills. From the beginnings of experimental psychology in the laboratory of Wilhelm Wundt in Leipzig, established in 1879, and later in the United States and in England,[1] attempts were made to objectify the manner in which individuals move, the speed with which they react, and the nature of movement perception. Although at times these early attempts at evaluating basic movement responses were actually attempts to discover basic psychomotor indices of intelligence, later nineteenth century researchers began to focus on how various motor skills were acquired, retained, and forgotten.

A second force during the nineteenth century also provided a basis for interest in motor skills, which is seen in the twentieth century in various parts of the world. The Industrial Revolution began to spawn factories in which increasing numbers of adults and youth were employed and compelled to use their manual skills with more intricacy than was required in the agrarian culture from which most of them had come.

A third scientific-historical trend occurring in the last century also contributed to contemporary interest and research in motor skill learning. Toward the end of the nineteenth century, Queletet in France, Galton and his student Pearson in England, and Hall, Cattell, Jastrow, and others in the United States, who were exploring the psychological parameters of human abilities, began not only to design statistical methods for weighing an individual's scores on a given test, but also to evolve techniques whereby such scores might be compared to mean scores on the same test collected from a large human population. Karl Pearson developed the useful statistical tool called "correlation," which allowed a comparison of the manner in which one test ranked a group of individuals to the ranking given the same group by a second test. The awareness that indices of human abilities might be contrasted in this manner led to the more complex and useful factor analytic tools developed during the early part of the twentieth century.

American psychologists who became interested in psychomotor skills before World War II were generally considered "functionalists" and were not usually closely aligned with either the current behavioristic or the gestaltic schools of psychology then battling for recognition and respect. Analyses of psychomotor skills during the first decades of the twentieth century generally focused on "useful" tasks including telegraphic skills, typewriting proficiency, handwriting, and the like.

---

[1] G. Stanley Hall started the first laboratory in the United States two years later.

During the decades immediately following World War I physical educators and those concerned with producing superior athletes in several parts of Europe and in the United States began to research and write about the variables which potentially influence motor skill learning. For example, in the 1920s laboratories were started in Leningrad and Moscow whose mission was to explore the psychological variables that influence athletic motor performance and learning.[2] In the physical education institutes at Leipzig and Berlin, laboratories were established for the exploration of motor skill as well as other problems dealing with the psychological parameters of physical activity.

At the same time a few physical educators in the United States began to engage in the scientific exploration of factors influencing the acquisition of skills. Prominent among them was Coleman Griffith, who published the text *Psychology of Coaching* and who headed the motor learning laboratory at the University of Illinois during the 1920s and '30s. During the 1930s John Lawther at Penn State and Clarence Ragsdale at the University of Wisconsin also founded laboratories in which to study motor performance and learning. Ragsdale's book (now out of print) entitled *The Psychology of Motor Learning*, one of the first texts in English containing a scientific approach to motor learning, was the precursor of the several books which were published on the same topic over thirty years later.

Robert Seashore and his students were also leaders in the exploration and assessment of motor skills during the late 1920s and the 1930s. They developed several batteries of tests of manual dexterity and rhythm which would purportedly evaluate the skills needed in industry.

In the 1930s and 1940s, interest also became focused on motor ability tests which would assess the emerging competences of infants, children, and youth. The test developed by Oseretsky in Russia in 1923 was modified in various countries, including the versions by Doll and Sloan in the United States. The Gesell developmental schedule, published in 1940, also contains numerous motor items, particularly at the lower age levels; in this it resembles the California Scale developed by Bayley in 1933.

Several of the so-called intelligence tests developed at this time for children contained numerous items requiring motor competence. The Stanford-Binet as well as the Merrill-Palmer scales are examples.

During and following World War II there was a resurgence of interest evidenced by increased research dealing with psychomotor skill and

[2] For a more detailed discussion of the world history of research into psychology in sport and motor learning, see Chapter 1, "A Brief History of Sport Psychology," in Miroslav Vanek and Bryant J. Cratty, *Psychology and the Superior Athlete* (New York: The Macmillan Co., 1970).

learning. Again, this interest was often tied closely to practical tasks such as the abilities needed by pilots, tracking skills useful in operating radar equipment, and other wartime tasks. More basic problems also undertaken by researchers during this period seemed to constitute a kind of "spin-off" from the more war-oriented skills. For example, Edwin Fleishman, who was initially concerned with visual-motor coordination necessary for operating an aircraft, began to explore more basic parameters of human motor performance and learning in numerous studies carried out during the late 1950s and the 1960s, investigations of gross motor skill, strength, and endurance, many of which contain findings which have important implications for physical educators and coaches.

In addition to Fleishman's factor analytic work during the past two decades and that of Franklin Henry, Drs. Robert and Carol Ammons in Montana, Drs. Edward and Ina Bilodeau at Tulane, and Karl U. Smith and his students in Wisconsin, few sustained programs of research have been conducted in the United States to explore the basic parameters of motor skill learning and performance. Many of the available data have come from rather piecemeal studies, often conducted as part of advanced-degree work and seldom followed by more penetrating efforts.

Presently there are few available middle-level theories based on qualitative data which deal with such potentially important topics as motor skill acquisition and retention, transfer of abilities between two or more movement tasks, and the influence of perceptual feedback. Indeed, initial theoretical efforts to explain such qualities as reaction time or the effects of varying types of practice schedules, as well as efforts to classify motor skills into various categories, are based on a narrow range of tasks and on data from a relatively small number of studies.

In summary, several practical, theoretical, and philosophical problems make it difficult to sort out available information about motor skill learning. Some of these conundrums will be explored in the pages which follow. They are briefly listed here:

1. Seldom has any large sustained government grant been awarded to support basic research in motor skill learning, particularly programs concentrating on movement accuracy and power of the larger muscles, which are of particular interest to physical educators.
2. It is difficult to determine exactly what constitutes a *motor* skill as contrasted to task performance in which verbal, perceptual, or cognitive abilities play an important part.
3. The absence of global and valid theoretical frameworks makes it difficult to consider some of the more basic problems in motor skill learning and retention.
4. Present numerous and at times disconnected research studies are often

the short-term projects of individual degree candidates rather than thorough explorations of important theoretical and/or practical questions.

Despite these limitations, physical educators may follow numerous practical guidelines when attempting to teach motor skills of various types to their students. We shall explore principles suggested by current and past research. While at times the findings produce conflicting results, certain areas have seen a large number of studies, for example, explorations of the influence of sensory feedback and practice schedules on motor performance and learning. A moderate amount of information is available concerning the influence of such factors as mental practice on skill learning, but we have relatively little information on such topics as long-term and short-term retention and the transfer of both simple and complex motor skill. Similarly difficult to locate are studies on the influence of the teacher's personality and teaching strategy on the acquisition of skill, and studies on the subtle interactions of intellectual competence and movement accuracy.

Before proceeding further, it is important to identify what is meant by "motor skill" and "motor learning" as contrasted to other types of skill and learning.

What Is a Motor Skill?

Most authorities use the label *motor skill* to refer to a task which includes the necessity on the part of the performer to move accurately and with strength and/or power in various combinations. In other words, the movement "output" of the individual is the most observable and apparently important quality of a motor task.

Within the past twenty years, however, more than one scholar has been confronted with the difficulty of determining to what exact degree an individual's final movement effort depends on his movement capabilities as contrasted to his ability to interpret, select, and otherwise organize various kinds of sensory information which may be present within the performance context. As a result, such terms as *perceptual-motor skill* and *sensory-motor performance* began to appear. While at times these terms have been misinterpreted,[3] in general they refer to the observation by many scholars that the performance of so-called motor skills indeed depends on the manner in which the individual interprets various components of the total situation in which he is acting, as well as on the accuracy and force of his actual efforts to move.

[3] Recently some less sophisticated scholars have expanded the term *perceptual-motor* to mean that movement activities will exert a causative effect on a wide variety of perceptual and intellectual abilities, including reading.

Other similarly hyphenated terms have signaled the awareness on the part of other writers that still other components of the personality interact in direct ways with motor skill learning. Even such apparently simple skills as writing a capital letter of the alphabet require the ability to arrange serially several component movements. Mental practice prior to, during, and after the performance of a skill similarly calls on so-called higher mental processes. Thus, some have written about what they term *cognitive-motor skills,* denoting the apparent observation that thought is often an integral part of the ability to perform.

Mental rehearsal of a skill invariably compels the individual to translate the problems inherent in performing a complex movement into verbal descriptions and word cues. Reflection on one's efforts between trials and often during performance itself also elicits either audible or subvocal verbalization on the part of the performer. At least one recent writer has made a case that reference in most cases should be made to what he terms *verbal-motor* skills, rather than simply labeling efforts at accurate and/or powerful movements *motor skills* (see Cratty, *Physical Expressions of Intelligence*).

In addition to the rather subtle difficulties of determining what components of the human personality form the final motor output of the individual, even more formidable problems are encountered when sketching in the outlines of what constitutes motor skill and motor skill learning. Definitions of motor skill usually stipulate that to label a movement *skillful* two criteria must be met: (1) the task must be reasonably complex, and thus (2) a period of learning is necessary to master it. However, these seemingly precise criteria start to break down when we consider that whether a movement requires learning on the part of the individual depends on whether he is mature or immature, is of above- or below-average intelligence, and has a sound nervous system or one which is less than adequate.[4]

Thus, the characteristic of a skillful movement or motor skill is that at least a minimal amount of practice has preceded the execution of the movement, or that some rehearsal is needed before the task can be performed. A motor skill is one which is, to the individual performing it, a reasonably complex or difficult undertaking, rather than a simple movement which could be performed well with no previous exposure or by practicing it only once.

---

[4] I once heard a woman afflicted with cerebral palsy (who possessed a master's degree in psychology) describe the anguish involved in simply taking a plate of soup from a stove to an adjacent table. She reported having to concentrate for many minutes on the subparts of the movement, precisely "programming" the manner in which she would later proceed.

Types of Motor Skills

In further attempts to clarify the dimensions of a motor skill, several writers have devised classification systems for various movement tasks. Observing that all motor skills do not resemble each other, scholars have proposed dichotomies that purportedly afford a more precise manner of considering the numerous kinds of human learned action patterns.[5]

For example, it has been suggested that some motor skills seem to be composed of two or more discrete parts, so that the final performance is seen as a number of discontinuous components rather than a free-flowing whole. Skills of this nature are labeled "discontinuous" in contrast to the more common "continuous" skill which appears more internally coherent, integrated, and smooth. Discontinuous skills may also be characterized by temporal inconsistency; that is, they may include rapid motions, hesitation, then one or more separate, slower motions. Continuous movements, on the other hand, are more difficult to separate into components, appearing as a smoother action when projected on a time continuum. Scholars interested in the retention of motor skill have suggested that the remarkable retention observed when many movement tasks are reperformed is due to this rhythmic quality.

Two other interesting classification systems have been applied to motor skill performance. Poulton has suggested that some skills may be classified as "open" and others "closed." Open skills require the performer to adjust his actions to unpredictable environmental circumstances; for example, on the tennis court an individual must gauge his movements to the unpredictable returns of his opponent. An example of closed skill, on the other hand, is the movement required of the tennis player when returning the ball after hitting it against the relatively predictable backstop.

I have proposed a third classification system for motor skill performance. Some skills are primarily based on cues, detected by the individual's sensory organs, which give information concerning events external to the body. Tasks involving visual information are an example. One may also postulate that other skills are performed without extensive reference to sensory information external to the body, while the individual's eyes are closed and his ears are rendered temporarily inoperative. Many simple actions typify this part of the dichotomy, as well as several well-learned complex actions; an adult may be able to write his name while blindfolded, for example.

[5] Separating truly human skills from those also seen in animals poses an even more interesting undertaking which to my knowledge has not been attempted at the time of this writing.

It should be obvious that skills within the "real" world are not easily classified within neat compartments. For example, what kind of skill is involved in tennis? The individual's strokes may be made with little attention to his opponent's reactions; his movements toward the ball, on the other hand, are vitally dependent on the movement cues given by the opponent. Thus, at one point he is engaging in what might be termed a closed skill (he returns the ball with little attention to his movements or to the ball, once he has decoded its course), yet as he moves into position to hit the ball he is certainly depending on external cues and unpredictable events, and the latter part of his actions might be classified as an open skill. The tennis serve is another example. While much of the serve seems to be classifiable as a continuous skill—sweeping the racket forward to contact the ball, along with the subtle step and weight shift— the act of throwing the ball into the air before intercepting it with the racket might be considered discrete from those which follow. The tennis serve, the football place-kick, and numerous other skills which could be mentioned appear to have some relatively discrete components as well as others which are rather fluid.

To circumvent these problems in attempting to classify skills, Knapp and others have suggested that while such classification systems are valid, an even more helpful way to study motor skill is to imagine several rather continuous scales on which skills may be projected. A skill may be placed on a scale denoting whether it is completely continuous in nature (riding a bicycle in place), whether it contains both continuous and discrete components (riding a bicycle while changing directions frequently as you ride through a neighborhood), or whether the skill appears entirely composed of discrete and separate parts.

Similarly, two other scales could be set up to denote whether a skill seems completely or only partially dependent on cues external to the performer. A third scale would describe whether a skill is dependent partially or totally on unexpected and unpredictable events, or whether its execution is entirely dependent on variables under the control of the performer.

The three-dimensional model in Figure 1.1 graphically depicts these three scales for the classification of motor skills. As you consider the model, keep the following points in mind:

1. Placing a given skill within a certain compartment can be done only with reference to a certain point in time, for as a skill is practiced, it is likely to shift along one or more of the scales. For example, as a foreigner learns to drive in Paris, more and more of the events to which he may be subjected become predictable, and the skill shifts from the open

Types of Motor Skills 9

toward the closed end of one of the scales represented. A similar shift would occur along the scale portraying the external versus internal skill dimension.

2. There are numerous other dimensions on which skills may be classified, such as whether the skills depend on qualities reflecting perceptual organization on the part of the performer, whether subtle verbal cues are important in their execution, and whether their performance reflects various combinations of intellectual abilities. Some of these other dimensions of skill are discussed in Chapters 7, 8, and 9.

3. The type of skill to be taught within the three classification systems depicted involves numerous specific and general implications for the learning, and thus the teaching, of the skill. For example, determining the relative success of a skill component may be easier when the skill is a discontinuous (discrete) one than when it is continuous. Skills which may be labeled "open" are probably more difficult to acquire, and thus

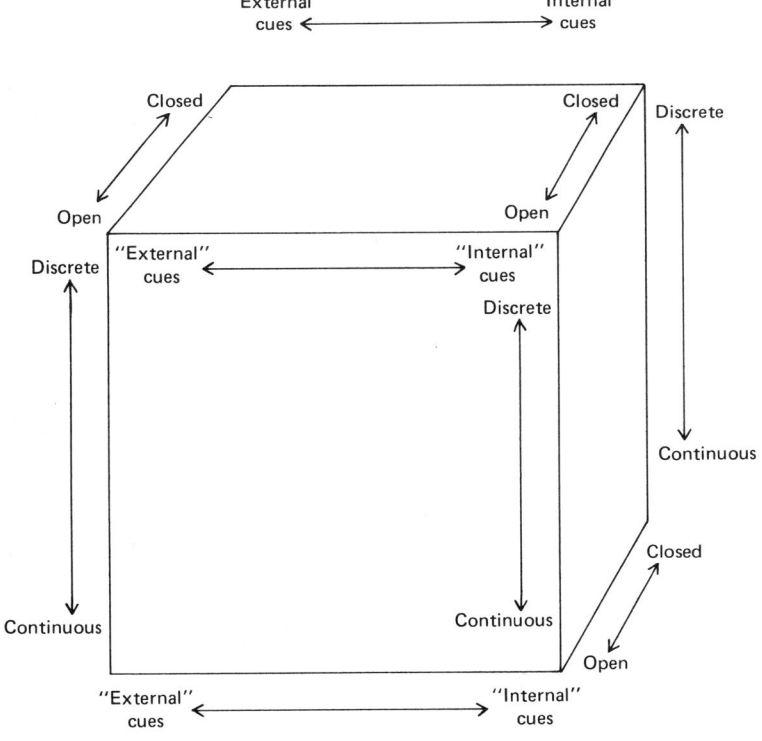

Figure 1.1 *Some dimensions of motor skills.*

to teach, than so-called "closed" skills. Skills dependent on external cues may likewise be learned, and thus taught, in different ways from those which depend on cues arising solely from the muscular system of the performer himself.

Perception and Motion

Terms such as *sensory-motor* and *perceptual-motor*[6] have also been attached to movement tasks, particularly in recent years. Programs that purportedly aid perceptual and intellectual development through movement, labeled "perceptual-motor education," have greatly proliferated during the past ten years. At other times the terms have been used to indicate that when a voluntary movement occurs for more than one second, there are probably identifiable and select perceptual and/or sensory components in the act whose effect can be studied.

Often the goals of various programs of perceptual-motor training have been dictated more by emotion, indeed by hysteria, than by reason, scholarship, and research data. What was said of the spurious principles and theories advanced in accompaniment to the various foreign programs of physical education imported to the United States over seventy years ago might also be said of most of the theoretical pronouncements accompanying programs of perceptual-motor education: "They are very simple, entirely logical, very superficial, delightfully fantastic, and mostly absurd."[7]

At the same time, the proliferation of such programs has focused the attention of many educators on other goals for and principles underlying programs of physical education in addition to the often stated goals of physical fitness, skill development, and social efficiency. We shall examine later some of the statements about possible intellectual and perceptual concomitants of motor skill development.

While the work of K. U. Smith and others has indicated that it is relatively easy to disrupt coordinated acts by modifying the spatial and/or temporal aspects of the task by changing the kind and quality of feedback afforded the performer, it is more difficult to prove that practicing various motor skills will increase the rather large number of intellectual and perceptual traits which have been identified by other scholars in the behavioral sciences (see Smith and Smith, *Perception and Motion*).

---

[6] Or even *motor-sensory* and *motor-perceptual!*

[7] Quoted from George W. Fitz, "Report of the Tenth Annual Meeting of the American Association for the Advancement of Physical Education," 1896, p. 178.

What Is Teaching?

The title of this book contains another deceptively simple term in addition to "motor skill." The meaning of the word *teaching*, obvious to many readers, deserves our close scrutiny before we discuss how teaching may be incorporated into an environment in which motor skills are assumed to be improvable. Many critical questions surround the interpretation and practical use of the concept of teaching in connection with motor skill improvement. For example, it is frequently noted that individuals improve their ability to perform various sports skills even in the absence of a teacher. Who is doing the teaching in such a situation? Can individuals teach themselves skills? If so, what skills are learned best by self-practice? What kinds of individuals are best left alone when practicing and which need help from another? Perhaps more important, if an individual seems to be teaching himself, how is this accomplished? Is he talking to himself? Is he visualizing the movement patterns to be employed? Or is he engaging is some kind of complex "feeling through" of the desired movement? The most important consideration is, how might teaching efforts be most effectively applied? Important questions concerning the timing and proper insertion of movement cues which will enhance, versus the presentation of cues which will possibly disrupt, the individual's efforts should be asked by the prospective teacher.

Historically, efforts to investigate what kinds of cues are important in the teaching and learning process have evolved through at least three phases. Around the turn of the century, psychologically oriented researchers often engaged in studies in which they and a single student participated. The two participants would sit across the table from each other and alternately attempt a task while transcribing their strategies and feelings about what was taking place. The final write-up of such a study was often rich in what were termed introspections (literally inspecting oneself) but at the same time lacking in scientific objectivity.

In the second phase of investigation, the vast majority of the studies of the influence of teaching and learning variables on motor skill acquisition have studied the effects of numerous variables (nature of the instruction, timing of trials, and so on) upon performances of groups of subjects. The results in these studies consisted of performance curves, usually indicative of improvement, obtained by averaging scores on successive trials. Thus, while many of the demands of scientific objectivism were met, the often erratic performance improvements and decrements recorded at each trial were usually not apparent, as the averages obtained tended to smooth out such irregularities.

During the latter part of the 1960s and the early 1970s the cycle seems to be turning again. Studies describing individual learning strategies in detail are again common. Similar to the "introspective recordings" in general design and approach, they differ, however, in the manner in which the performer's self-observations are obtained and recorded. Sophisticated electronic monitoring, not only of the performer's voiced strategies but also of the exact dimensions of his performances, efforts, and movement characteristics, has been achieved by coordinating voiced comments of the subjects with videotape representations of the performances and of the movement characteristics which accompany each attempt.

SUMMARY

Interest in and research about motor skill acquisition have occupied behavioral scientists since the middle of the last century. Their efforts have ranged from relatively primitive early studies whose findings were primarily arrived at by introspection to more sophisticated statistical efforts carried out more recently. At the same time, some of the more recent efforts have been marked by a return to the consideration of individual differences in learning strategies.

Other facets of the personality in addition to movement attributes contribute to the performance and learning of motor skill. The physical educator should acquaint himself not only with the manner in which verbal, intellectual, and perceptual qualities contribute to the acquisition of motor skill, but conversely with the ways in which participation in motor activities may potentially aid in the acquisition of other abilities in addition to motor skill.

Motor skills may be classified within several categories, according to whether they are discrete or continuous in nature whether their performance requires constant adjustment because of unpredictable outcomes of early parts performed (open skills), or whether the subject may perform continuously without any pronounced disruption of his efforts from events over which he has little control (closed skills). A third dichotomy divides skills into those which include tasks whose successful performance depends on some kind of information external to the individual (visual cues and the like), and those tasks which may be executed by the individual without reference to external cues.

Most motor skills do not fall at the extreme ends of the various classification systems, but somewhere along a continuum, combining, for example, elements which are "open" as well as other elements which are "closed." Other continua include a verbal-motor scale, which describes the degree to which verbalization contributes to the execution of a motor skill; a perceptual-motor scale, which pinpoints the manner in which various perceptual abilities contribute to performance; and an intellectual-motor scale, which describes the degree to which a skill contains intellectual elements and thus the degree to which the performance of the skill requires intellectual competences.

Intelligent teaching of motor skills cannot occur unless prospective instructors of physical skills understand the complexities of the behavior they hope to modify. The following chapter examines human motor performance; it should give the future teacher of physical education and motor skill acquisition a better perspective on the component of human personality he hopes to teach.

DISCUSSION QUESTIONS AND EXERCISES

1. Make a list of "open" skills and a list of "closed" skills. Might a skill move from one list to the other? What factors might cause such a transfer?
2. What different teaching methods might be needed to help students practice open and closed skills?
3. What is a perceptual-motor skill? What meanings can the term take on?
4. How might verbal behavior interact with motor skill learning?
5. How does motor learning differ from other types of learning?
6. How might verbal learning and motor learning be highly similar?
7. Analyze a complex sports skill different from those discussed in Chapter 1. Divide the skill into subcomponents. How might you relate your analysis to optimum practice conditions?
8. Discuss the interaction of internal and external cues as an individual attempts to learn a motor skill.

BIBLIOGRAPHY

ADAMS, JACK A., "A Closed-Loop Theory of Motor Learning," *J. of Motor Behavior*, III, No. 2 (June 1971), 111–50.

AMMONS, R. B., "Acquisition of Motor Skill: III. Effects of Initially Distributed Practice on Rotary Pursuit Performance," *J. Exp. Psych.*, XL (1950), 777.

BILODEAU, E. A., and BILODEAU, I. McD., "Motor-Skills Learning," *Ann. Rev. Psychol.*, XII (1961), 243–80.

CATTELL, J. M., "Mental Tests and Measurements," *Mind,* XV (1890), 373–80.

CRATTY, BRYANT J., "An Overview: Movement Considered Functionally," Chap. 19 in *Movement Behavior and Motor Learning* (2nd ed.). Philadelphia: Lea & Febiger, 1967.

———, "Feedback, Loops, and Servo-Systems," Chap. 4 in *Human Behavior: Exploring Educational Processes*. Wolfe City, Tex.: University Press, 1971.

———, *Physical Expressions of Intelligence*. Englewood Cliffs, N.J.: Prentice-Hall, Inc., 1972.

DOLL, E. A., ed., *The Oseretsky Tests of Motor Proficiency*. Minneapolis: Educational Testing Bureau, 1946.

FLEISHMAN, E. A., "Testing for Psychomotor Abilities by Means of Apparatus Tests," *Psychol. Bull.*, L (1953), 241–62.

———, "Dimensional Analysis of Psychomotor Abilities," *J. Exp. Psych.*, XLVII (1954), 437–54.

GALTON, F., *Inquiries into Human Faculty and its Development*. London: E. P. Dutton and Company, 1883.

GESELL, A., et al., *The First Five Years of Life*. New York: Harper & Row, Publishers, 1940.

GRIFFITH, COLEMAN, *Psychology of Coaching*. New York: Charles Scribner's Sons, 1926.

———, *Psychology and Athletics*. New York: Charles Scribner's Sons, 1928.

HENRY, FRANKLIN, "Increased Response Latency for Complicated Movements and a 'Memory Drum' Theory of Neuromotor Reaction," *Res. Quart.*, XXIII (1960), 448–57.

KNAPP, BARBARA, *Skill in Sport: Attainment of Proficiency*, p. 152. London: Routledge & Kegan Paul, 1963.

LAWTHER, JOHN, *Psychology of Coaching*. Englewood Cliffs, N.J.: Prentice-Hall, Inc., 1951.

LINDQUIST, E. L., "Study of the Cognitive Plan in the Acquisition of Complex Motor Skill," Final Report, Project No. 9-1-107, Grant No. OEG-9-70-0012(057). Washington, D.C.: U.S. Office of Education, 1971.

POULTON, E. C., "On Prediction in Skilled Movements," *Psychol. Bull.*, LIV (1957), 467–78.

SEASHORE, R. H., "Stanford Motor Skills Unit," *Psychol. Monographs*, XXXIX, No. 2 (Whole No. 178) (1928), 51–66.

———, "Individual Differences in Motor Skills," *J. Gen. Psychol.*, III (1930), 38–66.

SEASHORE, R. H., BUXTON, C. E., and MCCOLLOM, I. N., "Multiple Factorial Analysis of Fine Motor Skills," *Amer. J. Psychol.*, LIII (1942), 251–59.

SMITH, KARL U., and SMITH, WILLIAM M., *Perception and Motion*. Philadelphia: W. B. Saunders Company, 1962.

2

Motor Performance

Armed with information on how motor performance can be viewed, measured, and separated into component parts, the prospective teacher of physical skills is well equipped to become a careful observer and evaluator of motor behaviors, and to be better able to change the motor performance of those who seek his guidance. The so-called learning curves discussed in these chapters are really measures of successive performance changes. Thus, information about performance is vital to gaining an understanding of skill acquisition and the manner in which physical tasks may be taught successfully.

Motor performance can be considered a "bit" of behavior which most observers would characterize by saying that an individual is moving in various ways. The movement may be in relationship to some object or piece of equipment, or it may be independent of any environmental support except the ground. In addition, most definitions of motor performance imply that the results of the movement are measurable (for example, "How far did he jump?"), and that the observer can discern and the performer can describe the purpose of the act. Thus, a strict definition of motor performance tends to exclude subtle muscular tensions which are not readily observable and apparently random acts which seem to lack purpose.

Other categories of movement behaviors are difficult to classify within either of the above categories. For example, there are personal tendencies which seem to influence apparently well-structured and precise motor performance tasks. Gestures, bodily movements, and facial expressions are movements which may or may not be under the conscious control of the person emitting them, and depending on the circumstances they may or may not be easily measured. Moreover, a case could be made that all movements are caused by something, whether an internal emotional state of which the individual is not aware, or by external circumstances; thus, no observable movement could be designated as random and purposeless.

While it might seem that consideration of the various phases of movement behavior is extraneous to the study of skill teaching and acquisition, it is becoming increasingly apparent to those who purport to measure motor performance and performance changes precisely that a number of rather subtle factors "creep into" the data they collect and result in significant modifications of the outcomes they assess. Other facets of the individual's personality, including his verbal, perceptual, and intellectual capacities, influence the manner in which he applies force, moves accurately, and persists at his tasks when manifesting the action component of his personality.[1]

This information is not presented to confuse or complicate the nature of motor performance, but to illustrate to the reader the several factors, even within the "movement" part of the individual's personality, which can conceivably mold his final physical efforts, and which at times seem to counteract and confound the best attempts of the teacher-coach to improve skill proficiencies.

For example, several researchers have discovered what they term personal preferences for movement. Even when specific performance instructions are given by a teacher-coach, the performer's final efforts are molded by individual tendencies to move in various ways. Some individuals prefer to move rapidly in certain tasks, while others are slower. There are individual differences in rhythmic and space allowance preferences, too.

Fine and Gross Motor Skills

A common type of classification system is one in which some motor skills are classified as "fine" and others are termed "gross." This system implies that motor acts can be neatly divided into those which involve the larger muscle groups (gross), and those in which the smaller muscles

---

[1] For a more detailed discussion of this topic, see Bryant J. Cratty, *Human Behavior: Exploring Educational Processes* (Wolfe City, Tex.: University Press, 1971), particularly Chapters 3 and 4.

are employed (fine). At other times, the dichotomy seems to be based on the assumption that some skills require larger amounts of space than do others; or such a classification system divides skills according to the amount of force required for each.

Usually, it has been inferred that physical educators should be primarily concerned with the propagation of gross motor skills, while the fine motor skills are left to others, perhaps the industrial psychologist or the vocational therapist. However, a thorough consideration of the remarkable number and complexity of motor skills in which man is capable of engaging suggests that the neat fine-gross dyad should at least be expanded to include an intermediate level of skill; more accurately, skills should probably be located at various places along a fine-gross continuum.

A three-way classification divides skills into those which involve the large truncal muscles, in which the total body changes position in space; an intermediate level involving movements of the limbs; and a third level in which only the hands-fingers-wrists, for example, are moving. Such a triad seems to take into account both space and force dimensions of movement, for the larger muscles may exert more force and propel the body through larger amounts of space than do the smaller, and thus weaker, muscles and muscle groups.

However, once again a close look at muscular activities, including sports skills, reveals the difficulty of assigning a single label (fine, intermediate, gross) to most activities. Balance activities, while usually assigned a place within the "gross" category, actually involve rather finite adjustments of the muscle groups surrounding the feet and ankles, as well as the larger truncal and leg musculature. In the case of static posturing (see Fig. 2.7), the individual is indeed attempting to keep his body within a rather restricted space field. Most complex sports skills likewise require fine adjustment of the feet and hands, as the athlete attempts to run, intercept, and perhaps catch a ball thrown to him. Similarly, individuals confined to a desk and purportedly engaging in fine motor activity (such as typing or handwriting) frequently complain of backaches and similar discomfort involving the larger truncal muscles. Experimental evidence confirms that a great deal of activity takes place in the larger muscle groups even though an individual is apparently engaging in what most would term fine motor skills.

Thus, a closer look at most sports skills suggests that much of the time an individual's total muscular system is working in concert, large muscles may stabilize, while small muscles evidence forceful exertions; at other times subtle adjustments of the smaller muscle groups contribute to and enhance the efforts of the larger muscles working together in precise ways.

Figure 2.1 *A player dribbling a ball uses larger muscle groups to propel himself down the floow with accuracy (gross motor skill); his arms must be correctly positioned, one to dribble the ball and the second to aid his balance and integrate with leg movements (intermediate motor skill); and the fingers and wrists must be correctly placed on the ball at the apex of each bounce to sustain and modify the pathway of the ball as it is dribbled along the floor (fine motor skill).*

It would seem desirable for physical educators not only to familiarize themselves with movements in which the larger muscles are used to exert maximum force, but also to become aware of how the smaller muscles of the body cooperate, support, and otherwise contribute to sports skills. While the body may jump, the muscles of the hands must catch balls; while the sprinter may exert simple straightforward speed, the discus thrower must release his missile precisely; while the basketball player must be able to leap vigorously to great height, he must also be capable of a "light touch" while executing his jump-shot.

If physical educators graduating from the more scientifically based curricula purport to be "movement specialists," they should, in addition to providing expertise on the playground, also assist all teachers who are interested in some way in improving skilled performance of children and youth, whether it be in vocational shop programs or while practicing handwriting.

TYPOLOGY BASED ON A CONSIDERATION OF TASK COMPLEXITY

Several writers have attempted to classify motor skills according to their evident degree of complexity as they are performed. Rather than adhering to a clear-cut simple—complex dichotomy, they have placed various motor actions within four-part and even six-part typologies.

Both devising and considering such a hierarchical arrangement of skill are helpful academic as well as practical pursuits. Man is capable of a multitude of muscular actions; lending some kind of order to this apparent chaos should lead to a more helpful and organized way of teaching motor skills to others. The hierarchy presented here consists of a four-part breakdown.

Simple Movements

At the most elementary level are actions which may be termed *simple,* including simple and direct actions requiring no complex adjustment and involving only one part of the body, with the other parts relatively inactive or acting only as stabilizers. A direct arm movement, while seated, is an example. A simple straight-run for a short distance is another. Some would argue that such actions do not really constitute "skilled performance," but we must consider who is attempting to execute these simple actions. A young child, or someone with a damaged nervous system which limits the accuracy with which he moves might consider a straight-ahead ten-foot walk a highly skilled task indeed.[2]

Compound Tasks

At a second level are postulated a number of what might be termed *compound tasks,* which, while having simple components, are repetitive in nature and at times involve changing tempo or timing of movements chained together in various ways. An example of a compound task is running straight ahead, stopping, and then running again, for several repetitions. Another example would include repetitive but simple arm movements in time with a musical beat.

Complex Movements

Complex movements, which form the next and purportedly more difficult level of the hierarchy, are composed of two or more actions

---

[2] Note that our typology emphasizes the nature of the *movement,* not the judgments which might be necessary prior to and while executing the movement. For example, a computer programmer may actually be executing simple pushing movements on typewriter keys which in themselves are simple movements within our hierarchy, while at the same time which keys he chooses to push depends on complex cognitive and logical judgments.

which taken separately would be dissimilar in nature. An example is the underhand pitch in softball: a step forward (a "simple" task) and underhand and circular throwing movement executed simultaneously. Complex movements may be composed of more than two components, exemplified by the three- or four-stage tennis serve and the complex windup and delivery of the baseball pitcher.

In complex movements the body may travel through space, as in some of the more advanced springboard dives, or it may remain relatively fixed while numerous integrated movements take place within the truncal and/or limb musculature, as in some of the more modern dance movements executed with the feet held rigidly in place.

The final category contain what are termed *skill families.* Within this subdivision are groups of skills which are employed together to execute a number of jobs such as those seen in industry, in games played on the athletic field, and in musical accompaniment provided by orchestras. For example, the variety of running behaviors, throwing actions, and catching and fielding stances seen on the baseball field together constitute a skill family. Likewise, the several skills needed by the bass player in the orchestra constitute another family: bowing, plucking the strings, and so on. Numerous other skill families are seen in various industrial contexts. The drill press operator must be skilled in several tasks, rather than in only a single one, to carry out his job effectively.

To be an effective teacher or coach, one must recognize several principles implied within this typology:

1. Be aware of the level of complexity of a given skill, taking into consideration the maturity, background, and competences of the learner. Become aware of the level at which a learner may be introduced to a given skill family. Younger, less able learners, for example, may need to approach the more basic parts before attempting to master the complex or compounded wholes. More able performers need not spend time in the pursuit of the same skill basics.
2. Be aware of the nature of lead-up skills, located at lower levels within the typology, which relate to the more complex levels, the compound skills and skill families. Basic movements at the more simple levels undergird and support those at the more advanced levels. Your awareness of these supports and of how they may be taught to the learner should contribute to his acquisition of movements at the more complex and difficult levels.
3. Be aware of a learner's past experience, and assess the demands of the skill family confronting him. The perceptive teacher should be able to identify which members of the family presently under consideration are also members of a previous skill grouping which the learner may already have mastered. Previous acquisition of skill elements present in more

than one skill grouping probably enhances the later learning of sports skills by more experienced performers.

SKILL FAMILIES
All the skills in volleyball, baseball, and the like
COMPLEX MOVEMENTS
Two or more "stage" skills, such as baseball pitch, volleyball serve, and basketball jump shot
COMPOUND TASKS
Rhythmic but similar movements chained together, such as skipping, running a zigzag pattern, bouncing a ball
SIMPLE MOVEMENT
Simple jump forward or upward; forceful striking movement, one motion in response to a sound cue

Figure 2.2 *Illustration of a typology of motor skill.*

Physical Ability Traits: Their Identification and Implications

Divining the basic nature of the human personality, judging from the writings of the ancient Greeks and Romans, has long been considered a respectable scholarly undertaking. Not until the latter part of the last century, however, was the analysis of human abilities carried out with anything resembling a scientific approach.

Concerned with the basic nature of human intelligence, Sir Francis Galton and his young student Karl Pearson in England, as well as McKeen Cattell in the United States, Wilhelm Wundt, the father of experimental psychology, in Germany, and others, began not only to devise tests to evaluate intellectual and perceptual as well as sensory-motor capacities in individuals, but also to explore the manner in which the scores of an individual differed from the average. Most important, they began, with the then new technique termed *correlation,* to explore how groups of people seemed to rank themselves from the most to least proficient in two or more tests they had taken.

Among their early discoveries was the finding that basic sensory-motor tests were not very helpful in predicting how individuals might rank in tests evaluating so-called "higher" intellectual processes involving memory, vocabulary, application of principles, and the like; moreover, they began to discover that not only were most groups of intelligence scores not related to motor capacities, but that intelligence scores obtained from more than one test were also often not related to each other!

These findings, rather disquieting to some, provided the impetus for a more advanced statistical technique, *factor analysis,* which emerged in the early part of this century. Additionally, by the 1930s factor analysis, or what some might term "correlations of correlations," began to be applied to the dissection of motor skill performance.

It was discovered early that to a large degree, proficiency in tasks involving manual dexterity was not related to proficiency in tasks in which larger muscle groups were employed. Additionally, it began to be perceived that even tasks which were superficially similar often did not fall within the same basic group when subjected to factor analytic methods.

Essentially, factor analysis is a statistical tool (now many-faceted) which attempts to identify from scores on a number of tests given to a large group of subjects, a relatively small number of basic qualities which are common to two or more of the tests in the battery, and which, conversely, may, given the manner in which a single test score ranks people, determine what basic qualities seem to contribute to performance of that single test.

Thus, in one sense factors represent clusters of test scores. If, for example, our test battery consists of twenty tests, and five seem to intercorrelate to a moderate or marked degree, we say that we have identified at least one cluster of scores, or *factor.* Similarly, if within this same battery an additional six tests cluster, we have identified a second factor. These separate factor scores would be expected to correlate very low with each other, and thus would probably represent two rather independent abilities.[3]

The outcome of a factor analysis is a series of numbers (correlation coefficients) listed in separate columns, each column representing the degree to which each test score correlates with the different, rather global factors. The numbers are termed *factor loadings.*

---

[3] Usually one or more tests in such a battery do not correlate with any of the other tests; it is hypothesized that each such test evaluates an attribute which is not common to any of the other tests in the battery, but instead samples some unique and independent quality in the individuals tested. Such a failure to load in a factor with other tests would be expected if a test of "vocabulary" were placed within a battery of motor ability tests and administered to normal children.

Table 2.1 Factor loadings emerging from a factor analysis of physical ability tests.

Factor I		Factor II		Factor III		Factor IV	
Test #2	.68	Test #7	.50	Test #3	.65	Test #5	.65
Test #4	.48	Test #8	.48	Test #1	.55	Test #11	.56
Test #6	.40	Test #9	.36	Test #10	.36	Test #12	.54
Test #7	.30						

Test #1: steadiness-aiming
Test #2: push-ups
Test #3: target throwing
Test #4: dumbbell curl
Test #5: foot-tapping speed
Test #6: chin-ups
Test #7: sit-ups
Test #8: back extensions
Test #9: reverse sit-ups
Test #10: rotary pursuit
Test #11: arm movement speed
Test #12: hand-tapping speed

Note: Factors are "named" by the investigator upon inspecting what common elements are apparently contained in the groups of tests which "cluster" or load within a given factor. Thus, in the above example, Factor I might be termed "shoulder-girdle strength," Factor II, "trunk strength," Factor III, "hand-eye coordination," and Factor IV, "hand-foot speed."

In Table 2.1, Test #2 (push-ups) correlates 0.68 with whatever is common to the tests "clustering" in Factor I, while Test #7 (sit-ups) 0.50 into Factor II. To evaluate the degree to which a given test contributes to the total factor we square the loading, for example, $0.50^2 = 25\%$, which basically means that whatever the total qualities (100%) influence the ranking of people in the total factor, 25% is contributed by the qualities which influence how people rank in the test of sit-ups.

Test #7 (sit-ups) loads into more than one factor. Thus, an index number of how much of the performance on each test (in this case, sit-ups) can be accounted for by the common factors in a given analysis, may be obtained by computing the test's communality. In other words, not only does a score on a given test contribute to varying degrees to the total factor in which it resides, but the converse is also true: the common factor contributes to that same degree (indicated by the factor loading) to the manner in which people rank themselves while performing the given test. Thus, the loadings of 0.50 in Factor II and 0.30 in Factor I indicate that the performance of sit-ups is contributed to by an attribute which we have termed "abdominal strength" (25%) and one which was termed "shoulder-girdle strength" ($.30^2 = 9\%$). We have now accounted for 34% of whatever seems to contribute to the ability to perform sit-ups.

Similarly, we might have inserted into our battery the minutes played by each member of a football team as indicative of the relative success and, by inference, the football proficiency of each team player. We might thus determine what factors seem to contribute to the ability to gain playing minutes in football.

A great deal of judgment must be used when interpreting data from factor analyses. For example, one must carefully examine the nature of the battery of tests and their composition and administration when attempting to deduce the validity of the outcomes of such a study. At the same time, the experimenter, after inspecting the qualities which are apparently common to the two or more tests "loading" into a common factor, decides the name of the factor. His subjective judgment when selecting tests as well as when naming the factors plays a major role in the conclusions derived from this kind of investigation.

Two other major variables should be carefully considered in any attempt to interpret a factor analysis: the nature of the subject population, and the particular factor analytic method employed when treating the data. For example, it is usually found that fewer discrete and independent factors will emerge when the subjects are less mature and/or less able intellectually than when the subject population is mature and intellectually capable. Much of the work reviewed in the pages which follow is taken from studies in which mature air force cadets were used as subjects, such studies are likely to yield a different type of factor structure than if a population of retarded children had been exposed to a similar battery of tests.

Although an extensive amount of work in statistical analysis was carried out in the 1950s by Edwin Fleishman and his colleagues, (it was suggested during the early 1960s that their research using factor analytic techniques was less than appropriate. Among the arguments was the suggestion that factor analysis should be employed only in an exploratory manner, that deciding upon the existence of rather precise ability traits is not an appropriate use of this statistical tool. Interpretation of the arguments requires an extensive background not only in statistics but also in the uses and interpretations of factor analysis, but it is clear that the techniques which purportedly identify basic motor ability traits are not without critics.

In summary, factor analysis is a statistical tool with which it is supposedly possible to identify common performance abilities, or elements common to two or more tests within a battery of tests. Conversely, given a motor performance test, it is possible, using factor analysis, to identify factors which may underlie and contribute to its performance.[4]

The following paragraphs will identify some of the more striking divisions of motor performance (ability traits) uncovered by researchers during the past thirty years.

Figure 2.3 gives a general summary of motor ability factors resulting from the work of Fleishman and others since World War II. The factors have been arbitrarily placed within two large subdivisions: (1) those which involve movements of the larger muscles of the body, and (2) those which involve manipulative activities. Within these two divisions, the factors have been further arranged so that they fall into various subgroups. Within division (1) are factors reflecting speed and agility, factors involving manifestations of strength and endurance, and a "balance group." The factors reflecting manual abilities—division (2)—have been arranged in rough order along a continuum, from those which involve relatively simple actions and reactions to those which are more complex in nature and involve perceptual judgments of various kinds.

Several of the factors contain tasks which are highly similar; these pairings have been connected by dotted lines. For example, the measures of dynamic strength are similar to those involving short exertions, which merely take place over a more prolonged period of time than the measures of dynamic strength. Similarly, measures of limb speed are similar to measures of dynamic strength; however, the former involve "unloaded" limbs (not holding anything heavy), while the latter often involve rapid limb movement against resistance.

It may be incorrect to discuss "coordination" in general or even to consider strength or balance as rather global qualities. Rather, in the case of mature males there seem to be at least four fairly independent kinds of strength qualities and at least four balance qualities, derived from tests which are not correlated with each other. The implications of these hypotheses will be discussed at the end of this section.

Figures 2.4, 2.5, 2.6, 2.7, 2.8, and 2.9 further clarify the types of tests which contribute most to the qualities outlined in Figure 2.3. They illustrate tasks whose performance contributes to the factors named in Figure 2.3. For example, two types of flexibility tests (qualities) are shown in Figure 2.4: slow, sustained effort to demonstrate range of movement, and rapid effort through a range of movement. Developmental as

---

[4] The mathematically able reader can obtain a more thorough grounding in factor analysis by consulting the tests by Harmon (*Modern Factor Analysis*) and Cattell (*Factor Analysis*).

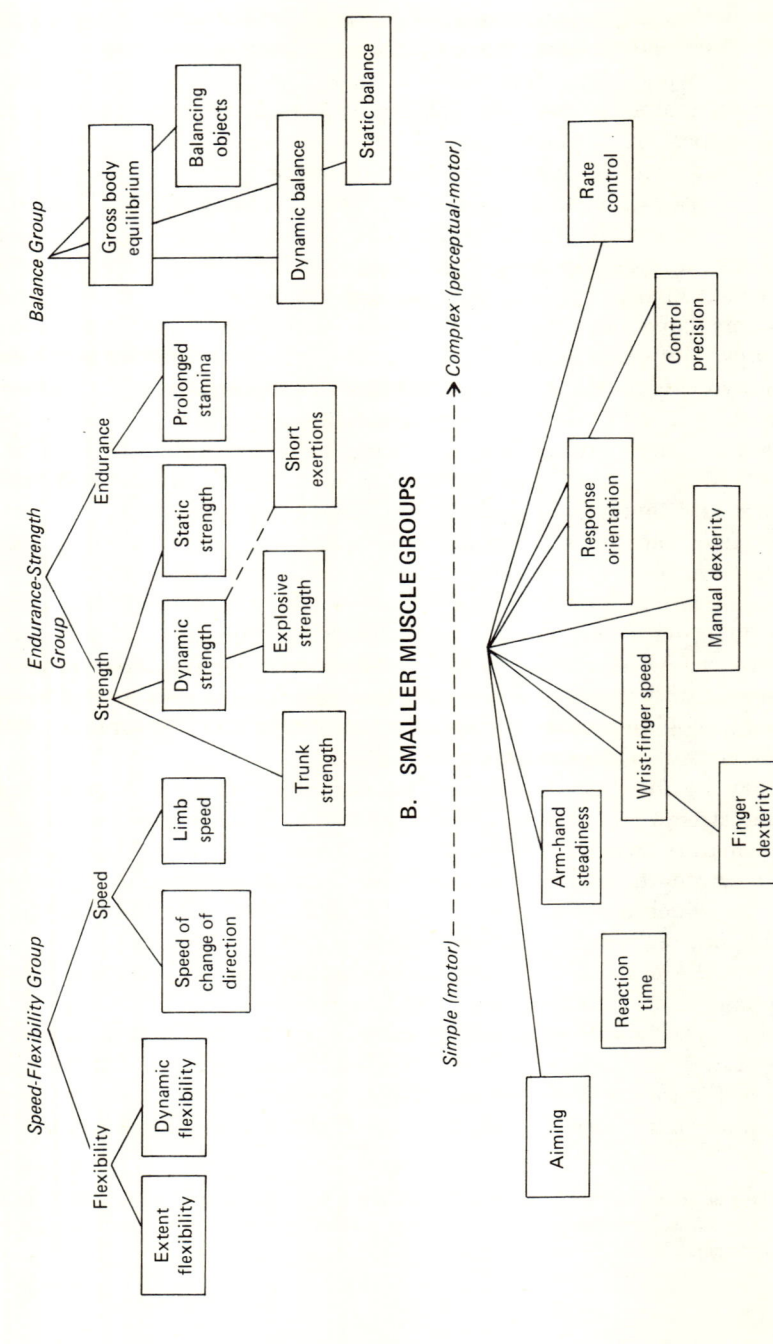

Figure 2.3 *Motor ability traits. Based on analysis of tasks employing (a) larger muscles of body, and (b) smaller muscle groups.*

Figure 2.4

well as other correlative studies indicate that flexibility measures gained from various joints in the body may not correlate highly; thus, an individual who requires or wishes flexibility improvement should be evaluated specifically before a rather blanket program of exercises can be prescribed.

The speed family of abilities, shown in Figure 2.5, also demonstrates more complexity than is normally assumed. However, there does seem to be a general speed-of-limb factor in tasks in which both the upper and lower limbs are involved. This factor might account for the common observation that good throwers may often kick well. However, we cannot simply assume that because an individual moves his limbs rapidly, he will also be able to move his whole body rapidly from place to place. Other research has indicated that the speed with which an individual *prefers* to move his body (to walk, for example) will not correlate highly with the measures of so-called "all-out" effort, upon which these factors are purportedly based.

Note also that speed and strength factors are highly independent, a finding which is at sharp odds with training programs that supposedly enhance throwing behaviors by exposing athletes to slow strength–producing activities either similar to or different from the throwing action itself.

The numerous "strengths" illustrated in Figure 2.6 indicate that any general kind of strength-training program should be comprehensive, including practice to enhance both moving and static strength; if ballistic or explosive strength is needed, yet another type of activity should be provided. Further research has also indicated that even static strength measures obtained from various parts of the body will often evidence only moderate or low correlations.

Developmental programs designed for young children often contain tasks to enhance balance. Again, however, the balance quality does not seem to be a simple singular. Although there is a likelihood of more generality of balance in younger children, by adolescence at least four types of balance qualities must be considered. The ability trait named "gross body equilibrium" in Figure 2.7 is actually contributed to by measures of static balance in which the eyes are closed.

Observation of activities like skateboarding, bicycling, and surfboarding hints at the existence of another, more complex balance factor, besides those identified by Fleishman, involving statically positioning oneself on a surface which itself is moving. Figure 2.7, however, does argue against a great deal of transfer from training in one kind of balance task (dynamic balance) to performance in another (static balance, for example). Similarly, learning to balance objects is not likely to enhance the ability to better posture one's body, either moving or static.

Figure 2.5

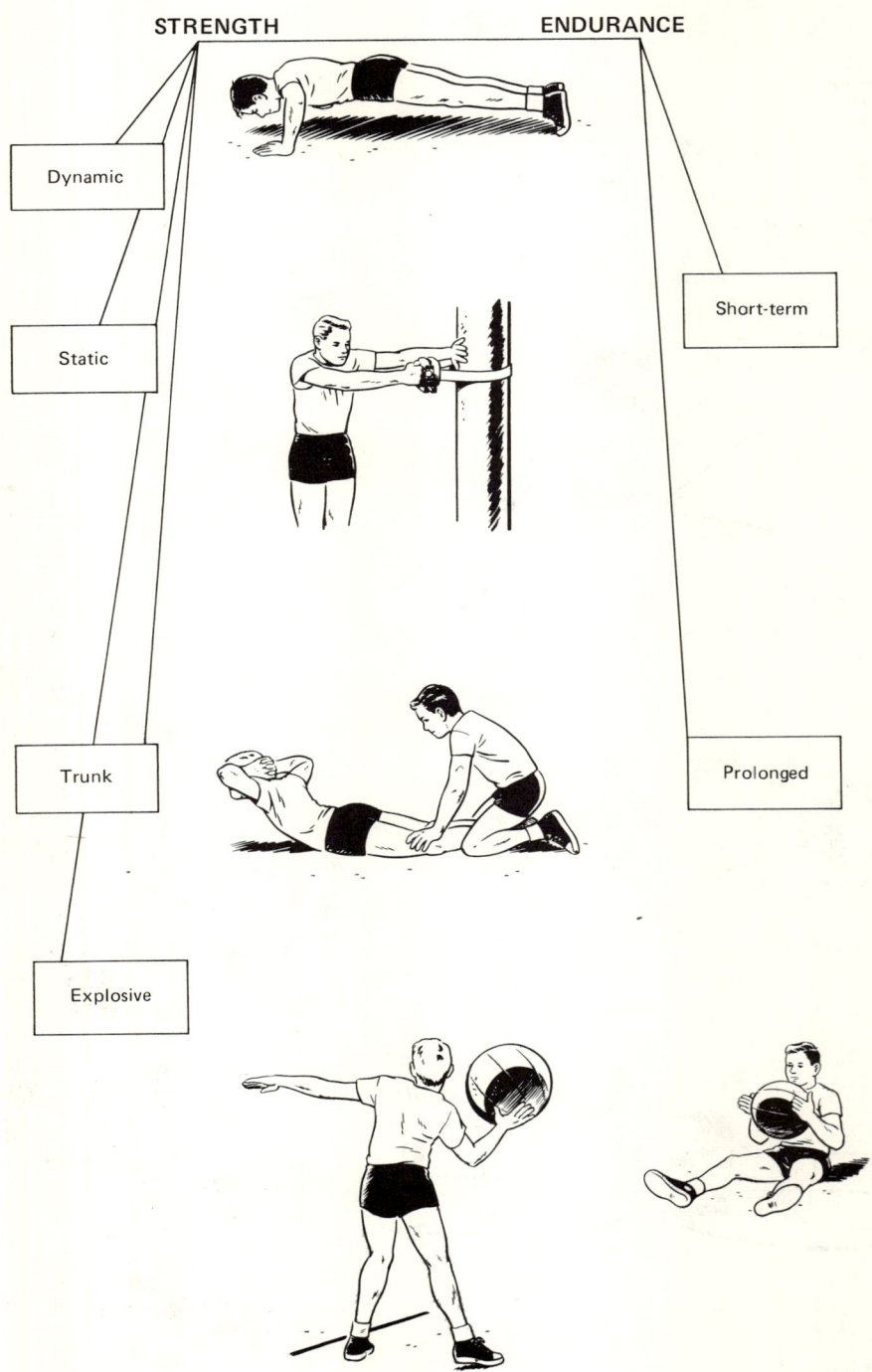

Figure 2.6 *Strength-endurance group.*

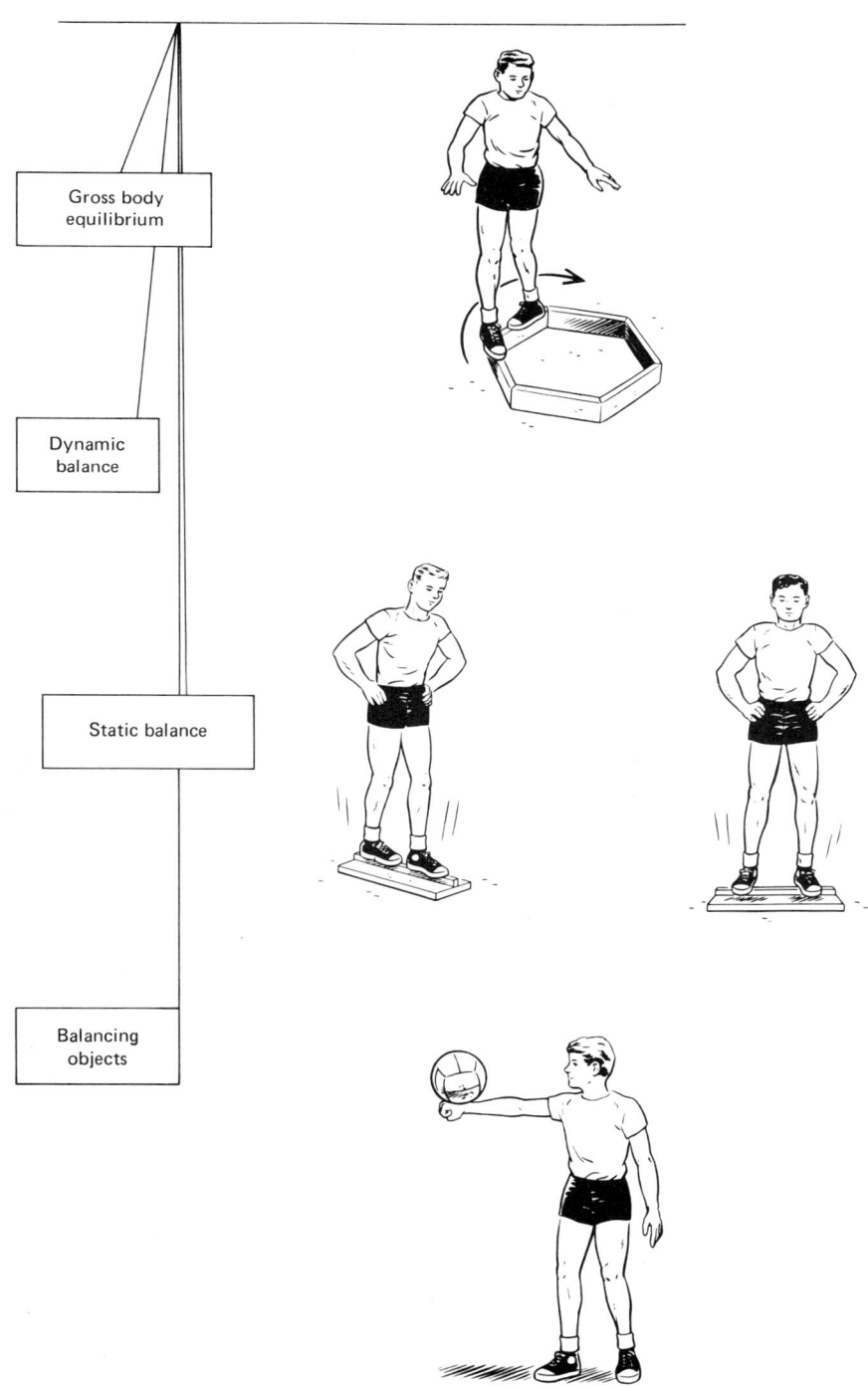

Figure 2.7 *Balance group.*

Figures 2.8 and 2.9 depict several manual abilities (fine motor abilities), which have resulted from exposing hundreds of subjects to dozens of tasks. Again, the data suggest that considering manual dexterity to be a single simple quality may be less than productive, both in analyzing tasks and in devising training programs. If we consider Fleishman's work statistically and experimentally valid, we must consider the existence of at least seven separate factors. For convenience, these have been separated into two groups; Figure 2.8 contains factors derived from intercorrelation of simple tests of reaction time, aiming, and the like, while Figure 2.9 contains those in which more complex perceptual subabilities are probably needed.

Acceptance of the philosophical premises upon which Fleishman's factor analytic research is based, together with comfort in the statistical methodology employed, has two rather critical implications for the teaching of motor skills, some of which are listed here:[5]

1. Before attempting to improve performance in a complex motor skill, determine what basic factors might contribute to the performance of the skill under consideration, and assess the feasibility and worth of attempting to improve these basic qualities before exposing the learner directly to the task at hand.
2. Training programs, particularly for able, mature individuals, should be comprehensive and should include several categories of tasks. Expecting transfer from a few so-called "general coordination exercises" to more complex tasks is less than realistic in view of research (see Chapter 8).

Reaction Time, Movement Speed, Response Time

Experiments in reaction time occupied the first experimental psychologists in Germany and America before the turn of the century. Recently a number of physical educators and psychologists have carried out elaborate research contrasting reaction and movement speed and investigating various parameters of reaction and movement speed.

Although in common usage the term *reaction time* has several meanings, in strict scientific terminology reaction time is the time between a stimulus which will impel an overt reaction, and the initiation of that reaction. Thus, reaction time involves *no observable reaction* on the part of the performer, but is rather the period needed by the nervous system to intercept some kind of stimulus, to integrate the stimulus within the central nervous system, and to transmit the appropriate impulses to various muscular groups. The longest part of this three-phase period is the

---

[5] For other principles derived from factor analyses in which performance of complex tasks at various stages in the learning process has been employed, see Chapter 3.

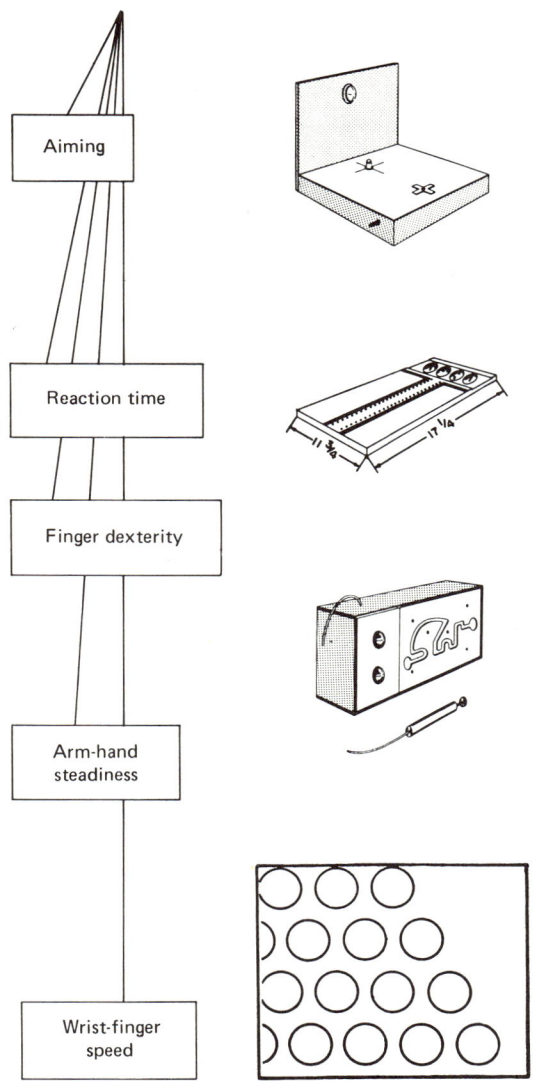

Figure 2.8 *(Small muscle) abilities—simple motor.* Reaction time test. *Subject presses button as rapidly as possible when light comes on. Score is the cumulated response times to the total series of signals.* Purdue peg board test. *Examinee is required to place pegs in holes, or to complete as many peg-washer-collar-washer assemblies as possible in the time allowed. Score is the number of pegs placed, or number of assemblies completed, in time period.* Track tracing test. *Subject inserts stylus in slot and moves it slowly and steadily at arm's length, trying not to hit sides or back of slot. Score is the number of errors (contacts) for the total trial.* Page section from "tapping test." *Examinee must make three pencil dots in each of a series of half-inch diameter circles working as rapidly as possible. Score is number of circles completed in time limit.*

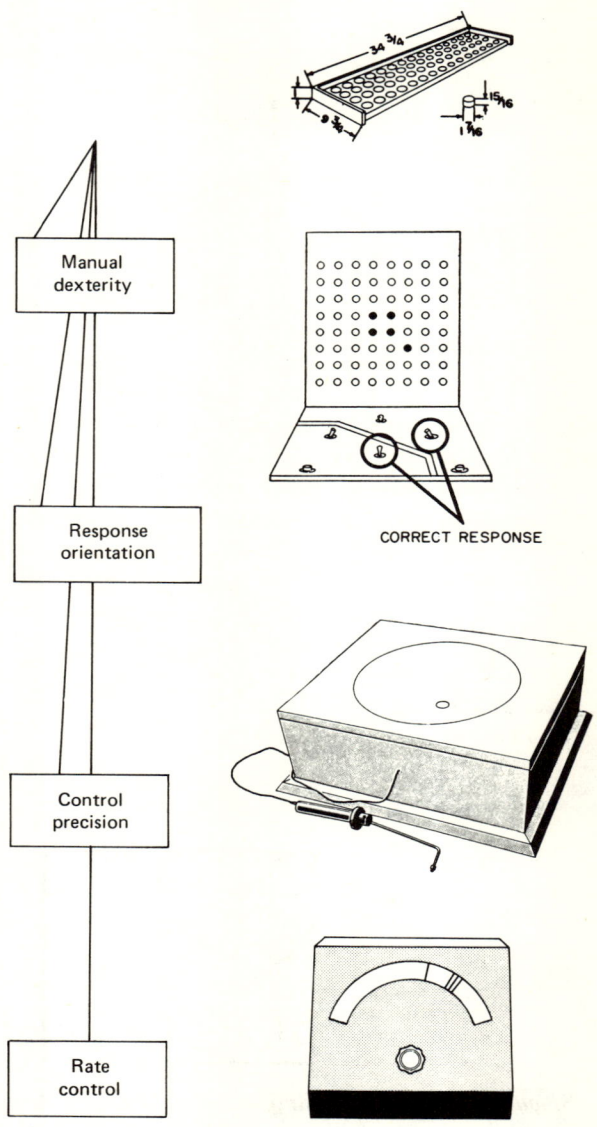

Figure 2.9 *(Small muscle)—complex motor abilities.* Minnesota rate of manipulation test. *Subject fills board with blocks, using one hand, as rapidly as possible; or he may be required to turn blocks over in their holes as rapidly as possible. Score is the time to complete task.* Rotary pursuit test. *Subject tries to keep stylus tip in contact with the target set near edge of revolving turntable. Score is total time "on target" during test period.* Rate control test. *Subject tries to keep hair line superimposed on target line as it deviates in unpredictable directions and rates. Score is time "on target."*

intermediate stage, integration time. *Movement speed,* on the other hand, is measured from the time a movement is commenced until it is terminated. *Response time* denotes the combination of both reaction time and movement speed.

Numerous variables have been researched as possible influences on the speed with which an individual can react. For example, not only the type of stimulus which triggers an action, but also the intensity of the stimulus, has been studied. In addition, the mental imagery employed by the performer while the stimulus is being expected has also been explored as influencing reaction time.

Reaction time may be divided into two broad categories: simple reaction time and complex reaction time. Simple reaction time is the time taken to initiate simple actions, usually upon presentation of simple stimulus conditions. Complex reaction time, on the other hand, is the time needed to initiate a rather complex movement response. It is probably best to consider reaction times along a continuum from those which involve a simple response, prepared in advance, to those which involve the sum of what might be termed *judgment time* and reaction time. Reaction times at the "long" end of the continuum involve prolonged periods of inaction during which the performer takes conscious measure of the conditions to which he is being exposed and selects from a number of possible reactions in response to these conditions.

Motor Performance—An Overview

The performance of a movement task is not an isolated event, but part of the total behavioral pattern of the individual. A person's performance of a given task will probably never be repeated exactly the same way, with the same force and results, and within the same spatial dimensions. Consideration of the unique nature of a "bit" of performance and of its apparent inseparability from the total personality of the individual gave rise a few years ago to the model in Table 2.2. This model has been elaborated on, and it is believed to present a fairly global, comprehensive view of motor performance and to hold several important implications for the prospective teacher and coach of physical education.

The model suggests that the numerous variables that potentially influence a single "piece" of motor performance may be considered within three large subdivisions: (1) basic behavioral supports, ingrained attributes which also mold other aspects of the individual's personality and abilities, including his intellectual, verbal, emotional-social, and perceptual functioning; (2) groups of ability traits, similar to those reviewed

Table 2.2 A three-level theory of motor behavior.

Basic behavioral supports	Ability traits and personal tendencies	Variables unique to the performance situation
Aspiration level Ability to analyze tasks General arousal level Muscular tension	Quality of strength factors Important perceptual abilities Reaction time Movement speed Flexibility factors Manual abilities	Previous practice in highly similar tasks Emotional climate Number of spectators Instructions before and during performance Motivation specific to the task

earlier in this chapter, combined with perceptual and intellectual traits which may affect the motor act in various ways (undoubtedly influenced by various personal preferences for movement); and (3) factors unique to the performance, occurring at a specified time and place, including the various aspects of the physical environment (temperature, humidity, wind), the emotional environment (the feelings of the performer about his performance that day, the reaction of onlookers), the amount, intensity, and recency of past practice in the specific task performed, and motivational factors which may momentarily impinge on the task situation and the individual executing the action.

The three levels of variables have different degrees of stability; as a result they are, within different limits, amenable to change by an instructor-coach. It is obvious, for example, that the variables within the third category may be changed more expeditiously by the teacher than those within the intermediate and the first categories. Various ability traits, together with the more basic modifiers of behavior, may be changed by the diligent efforts of instructor-coaches, but only if some time is devoted to their modification.

Variables within the three levels are not independent of each other. The quality of an individual "bit" of performance is weighed and "fed back" to influence the individual's general aspiration level and other basic supports of behavior, particularly if success or failure are prolonged or vivid. Similarly, the quality of performance, if high or at least encouraging, can result in more persistent practice which may influence the quality of ability traits possessed by an individual.[6]

[6] For an expanded discussion of this model and its integration with other facets of behavior, see Bryant J. Cratty, *Human Behavior: Exploring Educational Processes* (Wolfe City, Tex.: University Press, 1971).

DISCUSSION QUESTIONS AND EXERCISES

1. What is a motor ability trait? What are the implications of this concept for the teaching of motor skills?
2. In what sports is reaction time important? How might reaction time be improved?
3. Contrast the concepts of reaction time and movement speed. Which quality is more important in most sports skills?
4. Select a sports skill not illustrated in the chapter. Analyze its various subcomponents—fine, intermediate, and gross levels. How can such an analysis contribute to better instruction of motor skills?
5. Select a sport in which you are interested. Analyze it according to the typology outlined in Figure 2.2. Contrast your analysis with one of the same sport by another student.
6. How might your analysis in exercise 5 aid in the construction of a meaningful workout schedule for the sport?
7. Discuss motor ability traits, with particular emphasis on the role of preseason conditioning exercises in sports performance.
8. Discuss the three-level theory of motor behavior and its implications for the teaching of motor skills. Over what factors at what levels might the teacher-coach have the most influence? Which factors are not easily modified by a coach or teacher?
9. Contrast the ranking of ten classmates in a forty-yard dash with their ranking in number of sit-ups in fifteen seconds. Discuss your findings in relationship to concepts revolving around the specificity versus generality of human motor performance.

BIBLIOGRAPHY

BECHTOLDT, HAROLD P., "Motor Abilities in Studies of Motor Learning," in Leon E. Smith, ed., *Psychology of Motor Learning: Proceedings of C.I.C. Symposium on Psychology of Motor Learning.* Chicago: The Athletic Institute, 1970.

CATTELL, J., "Mental Tests and Measurements," *Mind,* XV (1890), 373–80.

CATTELL, R. B., *Factor Analysis.* New York: Harper & Row, Publishers, 1952.

CRATTY, BRYANT J., "A Three Level Theory of Perceptual-Motor Behavior," *Quest,* VI (May 1966), 3–10.

———, *Movement Behavior and Motor Learning* (2nd ed.). Philadelphia: Lea & Febiger, 1967.

———, *Physical Expressions of Intelligence.* Englewood Cliffs, N.J.: Prentice-Hall, Inc., 1972.

CUMBEE, F. Z., MEYER, M., and PETERSON, G., "Factorial Analysis of Motor Coordination Variables for Third and Fourth Grade Girls," *Res. Quart.*, XXVIII (1957), 100–108.

FITTS, PAUL M., and POSNER, MICHAEL I., *Human Performance*. Belmont, Calif.: Brooks/Cole Publishing Co., 1967.

FLEISHMAN, EDWIN A., *The Dimensions of Physical Fitness: The Nationwide Normative and Developmental Study of Basic Tests*, Technical Report 4. New Haven, Conn.: Yale University, Department of Industrial Administration and Department of Psychology, 1962.

———, *The Structure and Measurement of Physical Fitness*. Englewood Cliffs, N.J.: Prentice-Hall, Inc., 1962.

FLEISHMAN, EDWIN A., KREMER, ELMAR J., and SHOUP, GUY W., *The Dimensions of Physical Fitness: A Factor Analysis of Strength Tests*, Technical Report 2. New Haven, Conn.: Yale University, Department of Industrial Administration and Department of Psychology, 1961.

GALTON, FRANCIS, *Inquiries into Human Faculty and its Development*. London: E. P. Dutton and Company, 1883.

HARMON, H., *Modern Factor Analysis*. Chicago: University of Chicago Press, 1960.

SIMPSON, ELIZABETH JANE, *The Classification of Educational Objectives, Psychomotor Domain*. Washington, D.C.: U.S. Department of Health, Education and Welfare, Office of Education, 1965–66.

3

Acquiring Motor Skill

Definitions of motor learning usually imply that some kind of relatively permanent change of motor performance is taking place, primarily because of practice. Performance can change for other reasons also. Medications can radically alter movement characteristics, just as can unusual motivating circumstances or the ingestion of various nutrients.

Motor performance changes are usually depicted in research investigations by inscribing what are termed *learning curves*, curved lines made by connecting average performances of a group of subjects who took part in the studies. However, these curves may be misinterpreted. They are perhaps better labeled "performance curves," for they are *group descriptions of changes in average performance.* The relatively smooth appearance of such curves can be somewhat deceiving, particularly if one observes a single person engaged in the learning of a motor task. Individual efforts are usually marked by unexpected improvements and equally abrupt decreases in the quality of performance.

Additionally, it is highly probable that an individual may indeed be learning a motor skill without immediate confirmation in the form of improved performance. Subtle and unseen adjustments may be taking place within the nervous system of the learner, including changes in the way muscles and vision work together, or neurological adjustments, as the individual is exposed to a task—modifications which are not immediately manifested in measurable performance changes.

Several other important factors must be weighed when we consider the nature of skill acquisition. For example, which individuals seem to bring to a task situation a number of types of personal strategies, unique approaches to arranging the equipment and perceiving the environment, as well as personal choices to proceed cautiously and accurately or to try hard and to move rapidly during the initial attempts at the task. Individuals also choose whether trials are practiced close together or spaced apart; such preferences influence the nature of the performance curve.

Unique sets of perceptual, motor, and intellectual attributes also influence the shape of the performance curves after several trials of a task. Whether an individual evidences initial fast improvement or whether the best performance increases occur after several trials depend on these abilities which the individual already possesses.

Periods of no apparent improvement, marked by plateaus in motor learning curves, are often frustrating to both the performer and his mentor. Plateaus which may be encountered are important considerations when we devise practice programs, decide on appropriate instructions, and plan individual strategies for the acquisition of a motor task.

Several practical and theoretical questions should also be considered in a discussion of skill learning. For example, the concept of *motor educability* refers to the common assumption that some individuals are able to learn a variety of motor tasks quickly and well, and are thus highly educable in motor tasks. On the other hand, other people may have difficulty acquiring a larger variety of motor skills.

When the learner is gaining proficiency in motor skill, several types of changes are occurring which may or may not be reflected in measurable performance changes. Some of these factors are under the control of an instructor, some are not; some may be observed and some may not; however, all should be given careful consideration by those interested in teaching physical activities and motor skills.

1. Skill acquisition is usually accompanied after several trials by a reduction in muscular tension and effort needed to perform the same task.
2. Performance increases are apparent if the skill is not too difficult, or if limits have not been reached before the first practice session under observation.
3. Errors are gradually reduced as learning takes place. These may be *errors of commission* (doing the wrong thing, making the wrong move- or partial movement), or *errors of omission* (leaving out an essential movement or partial movement necessary for the smooth performance of the task).
4. Performance appears better integrated with practice. In the case of rhythmic movements, initial stops and starts grow smoother and compo-

nents of the movement are not as discrete in nature but appear to blend into each other, resulting in a smoothly flowing whole.

5. With practice the performer becomes better in the selection and interpretation of cues to which he must respond when performing a skill. Extraneous cues are ignored in favor of important stimuli, which are interpreted to an increasingly correct degree as the result of familiarity with the motor task. Not only are correct cues correctly selected out of many, but correct meanings are given to these cues. Moreover, the performer becomes increasingly able to anticipate what cues are important precursors of what subsequent actions.

For example, an experienced batter in baseball may not only become able to interpret correctly the nature of the pitch by observing how it is released by the pitcher, but with increased experience he may also become able to gain the same information by observing the wind-up, by observing how the ball is held as the wind-up occurs, or even by watching how the pitcher places his feet on the pitching rubber before the wind-up.

6. With increased practice performers may need to give less attention to both perceptual and motor components of the task. For example, with experience a child does not need to watch his arm during the throwing movement (less attention to a motor component); an older youth, after a few years' practice, may not need to watch a ball which is approaching him during its entire line of flight to be able to intercept its pathway correctly (less attention to a perceptual component).

7. As a result of the processes outlined in points 5 and 6, experience in a given motor task enables the learner to attend to an increasing number of potentially relevant cues while he performs. For example, the infielder in baseball may be able to take his eye from an approaching grounder and attend briefly to the progress of runners on the basepaths.

8. An increased number of motor components may also be incorporated into a complex task after increased proficiency is achieved in any one component. For example, an older child may be able not only to run, but simultaneously to place his hands in the correct position to catch, while a younger child must remain fixed while attempting to catch the first balls thrown in his direction.

9. Learning a motor skill can be divided into several time phases from an initial stage, usually marked by relatively rapid improvement; to later stages, characterized by plateaus, periods of less improvement, and irregularities due to motivational conditions and similar extraneous factors; and finally to a stage during which performance gradually declines because of boredom, fatigue, and similar variables.

Careful consideration of the nature of motor skill, its measurement, and the factors which modify skill improvement should make the reader a more careful observer of skill acquisition in himself and others. Careful observation of the behavior one hopes to modify, as well as thorough

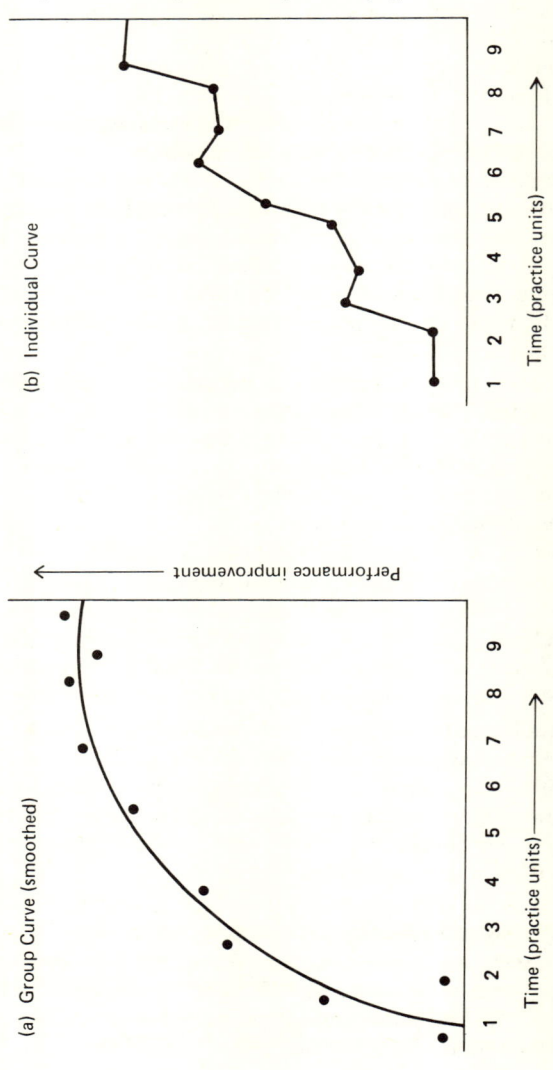

Figure 3.1 *Individual versus group performance curves.*

grounding in the scientific principles surrounding that behavior, should result in more effective teaching behavior.

Individual versus Group Performance Curves

In most research studies, learning or performance curves are depicted as in Figure 3.1(a). Because a large group of subjects are employed, the curce formed by connecting average performance increases tends to become smoothed; if the means do not fall within an exact curve, they may be mathematically smoothed. This gives the impression that performance increases occur at a monotonous, regular pace and in a highly predictable manner.

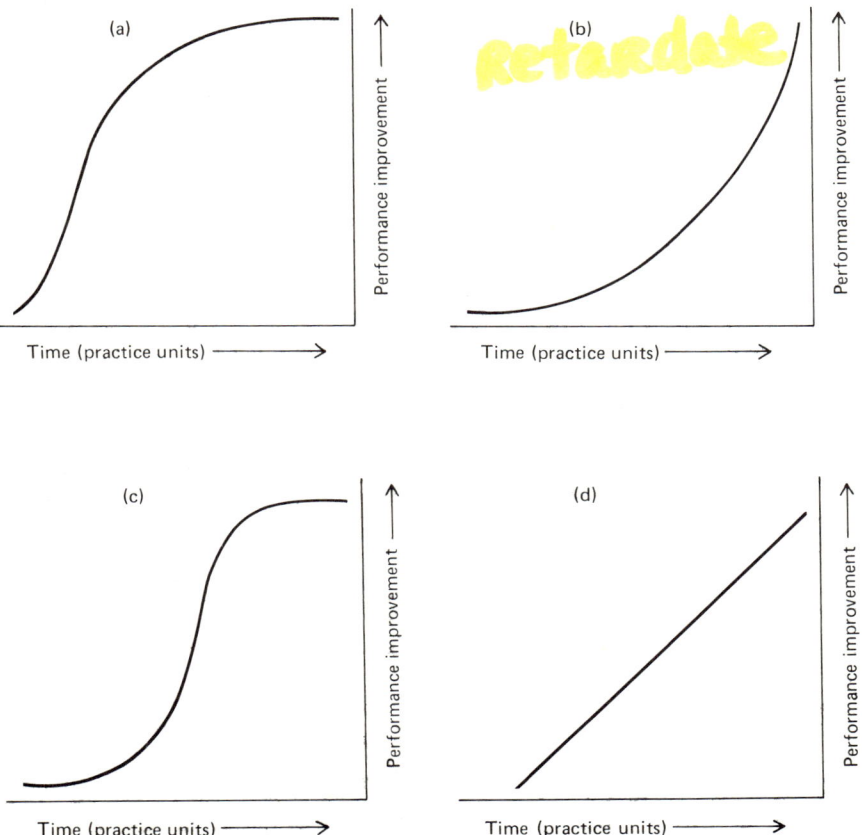

Figure 3.2 *Types of performance curves.*

In truth, however, an individual's progress at learning a motor skill occurs in the somewhat erratic manner graphed in Figure 3.1(b). The line connecting successive performance scores shows progress at times, at other times retrogression. Progress occurs as the learner acquires insight into the nature of the task or into techniques which enable him to improve his performance, as well as when his nervous system unconsciously accommodates to the demands placed upon it. Retrogression in performance may be caused by an even larger number of reasons: a decrease in motivation, boredom, physical fatigue, unaccountable change in task conditions, and/or a failure to keep attention focused on the task. Thus, a true individual performance curve appears very different from the mathematically "correct" performance curve of a group seen in most investigations of motor skill learning.

As in Figure 3.2 (a)–(d), individual and group performance curves may take a number of forms. Figure 3.2(a), for example, is a typical negatively accelerating curve, the most common result when progress in a motor skill is plotted. It is distinguished by marked improvement during the early stages and less improvement during the latter stages of skill acquisition.

A positively accelerating curve—Figure 3.2(b)—is less common, occurring when normal children are exposed to a difficult task or when retarded children or youth are attempting to acquire a task of moderate difficulty. Little progress during the initial stages of learning and then more marked progress result in a curve of the type shown. The more retarded a youngster, for example, the more trials he may need before he begins to attend to the task and before he perceives the methods needed to solve it.

Progress in skill acquisition may also appear in other forms. In Figure 3.2(c), for example, performance evidences first a positive acceleration and then a plateauing and negative acceleration. Figure 3.2(b) shows an unusual performance "curve" based on the highly improbable possibility that an individual could make regular and equal progress from trial to trial during the initial, intermediate, and later stages of skill acquisition.

An explanation for the occurrence of performance curves of the several conformations we have discussed is given in Figure 3.3. The assumption is made that the performance curve depicting the acquisition of a skill from birth through maturity to old age, if plotted completely, would resemble the kind of bell-shaped curve shown. During the initial exposure to the task, improvement would be slight; with experience and maturity, performance increases would be more marked; during the later stages of practice, when fatigue and boredom often set in, performance would

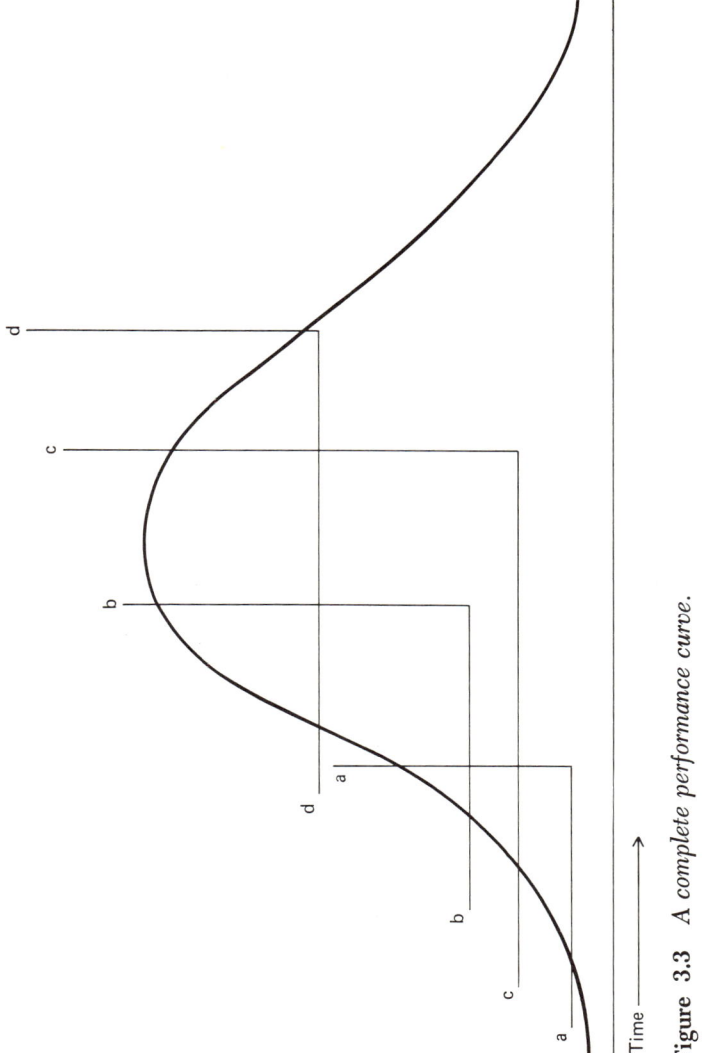

Figure 3.3 *A complete performance curve.*

decline until further confrontations with the task might elicit no performance at all from the individual.

Any performance curve obtained from a person might be conceived of as a section (a, b, c, or d) of this bell-shaped conformation. Section a is a positively accelerated curve from the initial stage of acquisition; section b is the negatively accelerated curve; section c, the compound curve, evidencing both negative and positive acceleration (quick as well as slow improvement); while section d might be obtained from an individual exposed to a too-familiar task which will quickly tax his interest, patience, and/or his intellect. The last type of curve, rarely seen in research, nevertheless should be considered by all instructors and coaches of physical activity. It is the picture of a football player fed up with the game, a stale tennis player, or an undermotivated basketball player toward the end of the season. Most literature dealing with the motivation of physical performers deals with the prevention of this type of curve.

Learning versus Performance

Most performance curves should also be viewed as concealing or at least as accompanied by unseen learning curves; that is, while performance may be plotted, true learning is not often apparent, either from observing an athlete or from carefully measuring his performance. As is obvious from Figure 3.4, performance parameters, depicted by the solid lines, may not coincide with the actual learning taking place on the part of an individual, depicted by the dashed lines. Learning may precede performance as in Figure 3.4(a), that is, an individual may not perform up to his actual acquired capacities during the initial stages of skill acquisition, and performance may markedly decline in later stages while learning remains relatively stable. This condition may be overcome when a "stale" or "plateauing" athlete is suddenly confronted with new incentives or allowed to rest for a prolonged period between trials (games), permitting some of his boredom to dissipate.

Performance may under other circumstances exceed true learning. Influenced by inordinately strong motivating conditions, an individual may literally be performing "over his head," evidencing performance which is not consolidated into true and permanent learning, as in Figure 3.4(b). Such a lag between performance and learning may become apparent when, upon removal of some kind of incentive or the interpolation of a period of rest, the individual does not exhibit competence in the task at anywhere near the level that he displayed in his first efforts.

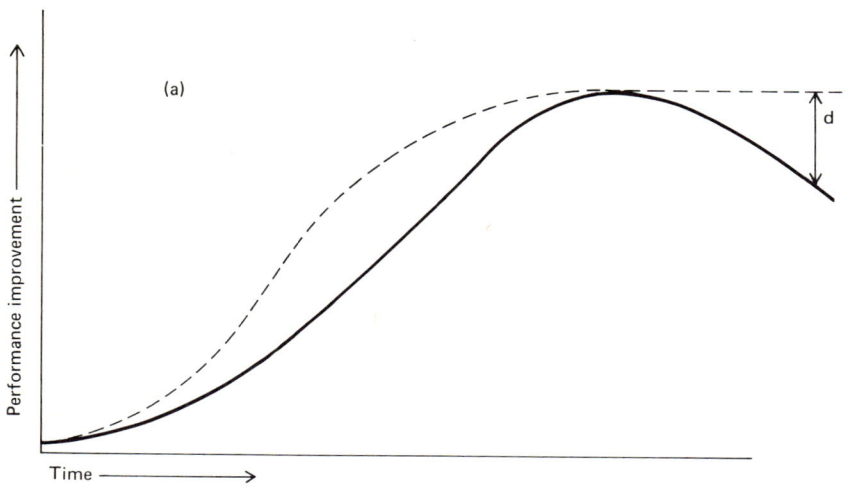

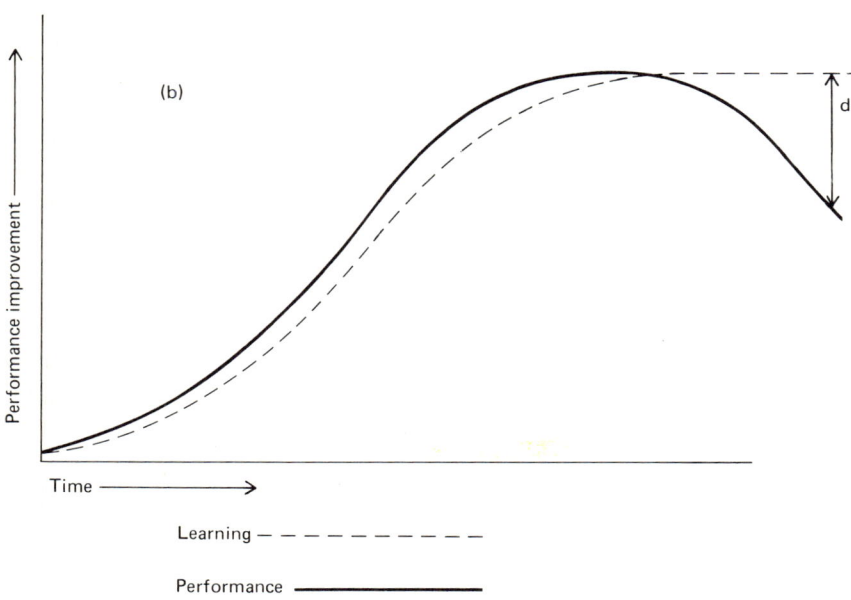

Figure 3.4 *Learning and performance compared.*

Skill Acquisition Over Time

Besides taking the various configurations previously discussed, an individual or group effort, over time, may fluctuate and vacillate through several reasonably predictable stages. For example (see Figure 3.5), the initial stages of learning a motor skill are often marked by early improvement, as the individual discovers similarities in performance strategies between the task at hand and previous ones to which he has been exposed. During this initial stage, instructions, either self-administered or emanating from another, may have rather marked effects, particularly if the instructions relate the task to previously learned and similar tasks. The second stage of learning is marked by less improvement and is felt by some to indicate a kind of consolidation period during which the task becomes well "stamped" on the nervous system. This period may also be marked by irregularities as interest rises and wanes, or as new strategies are experimented with and either adopted or rejected. A substage of this period is often marked by one or more plateaus in the performance or learning curve, periods of time during which little or no improvement may be recorded. The final stages of skill acquisition may be marked by one or more phenomena. Learning may evidence sudden spurts ahead as subtle processes are brought to bear upon the task at hand. For example, researchers have recently found that at advanced stages of skill acquisition the individual may unconsciously learn how better to pair his eye movements with the actions required, or he may acquire the ability to alternately hold, expel, and otherwise adjust his breathing patterns to the movements carried out within the requirements of the task. During this stage of learning, boredom and other signs of inhibition may also manifest themselves and the individual's performance efforts may begin to decline.

Motor Educability

Some individuals seem to learn a number of skills quickly while others have difficulty acquiring motor skills. The term *motor educability* denotes the possibility that some general learning-how-to-perform motor skill quality may be present to varying degrees within individuals; thus, an individual who seems to learn several skills quickly may be said to evidence a high degree of motor educability, while someone who apparently has difficulty learning motor skills rapidly would be said to exhibit a low level of motor educability.

Several researchers have attempted to determine whether some kind of general learning ability exists, and to identify this general quality in

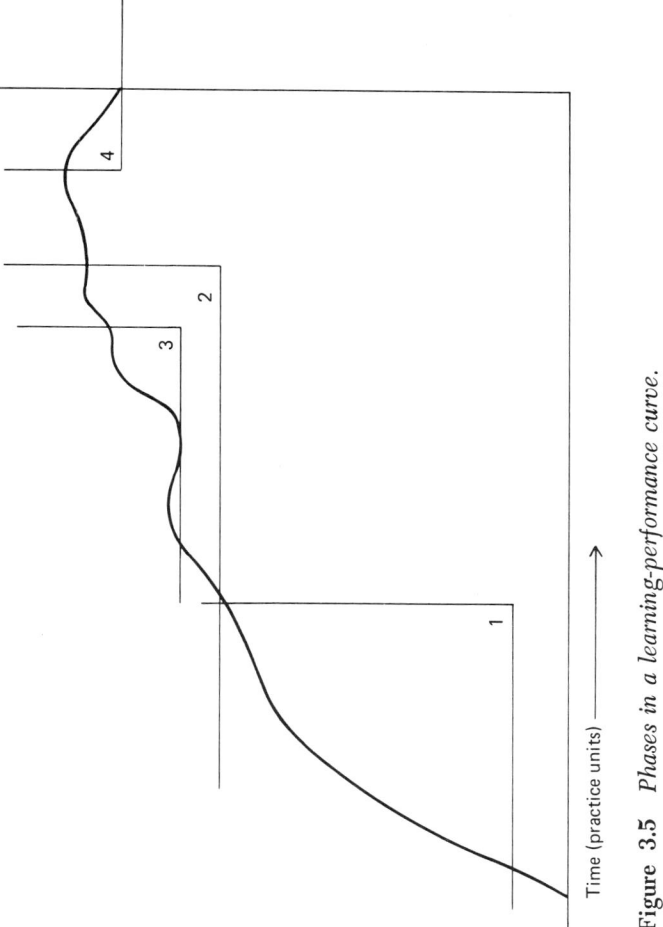

Figure 3.5 Phases in a learning-performance curve.

individuals. In research of this type, a large group of people are given numerous motor skills to learn, and then it is determined whether the degree of improvement in one motor skill may be predicted by inspecting their progress in others. In general, it is experimentally difficult to prove the existence of some kind of general ability to learn motor skills. Improvement in one skill is usually not predictable from knowing how an individual or a group of subjects performed in other skills.

It is highly possible that people we see perform well in more than one skill are exhibiting abilities in skills which are highly similar and whose similar components readily transfer from skill to skill; or they are motivated for some reason to spend an inordinate amount of time when confronted with more than one skill in attaining proficiencies which they may exhibit to others.

It is also possible that with increased familiarity with a great number of motor skills, some individuals acquire certain general qualities which enable them to acquire subsequent skills more readily. They may, for example, become able to analyze skills very well, to perceive readily what elements in the new skill are similar to those in past skills practiced, and they may transfer past experience with increased facility. (The acquisition of general learning sets will be dealt with in more detail in Chapter 8.)

In general, however, the ability to learn a motor skill seems highly specific to individual skills. Little or no general motor educability has been identified in the few previous studies on this topic. Several reasons might be hypothesized for the apparent specificity of skill learning: (1) motor performance may be highly specific, making acquisition of motor performance similarly specific to the task; (2) the skills researched in motor educability studies may have been for the most part composed of dissimilar elements; (3) as shown in Figure 3.6, the time within which an individual or a group of subjects is exposed to a group of tasks within an experiment is relatively short in comparison with their total experience with motor skill acquisition. It is likely that during the relatively brief period of testing, some of the skills sampled have already plateaued, due to their similarity to past motor acts with which the individuals have been confronted since birth; others may be undergoing rather rapid rates of improvement during the time they are sampled within an experimental setting, thus accounting for the rather low correlations obtained in such studies when improvement in several skills is contrasted.

The Measurement of Motor Learning

Numerous formulas may be employed when evaluating motor skill improvement based upon successive performance increments. For exam-

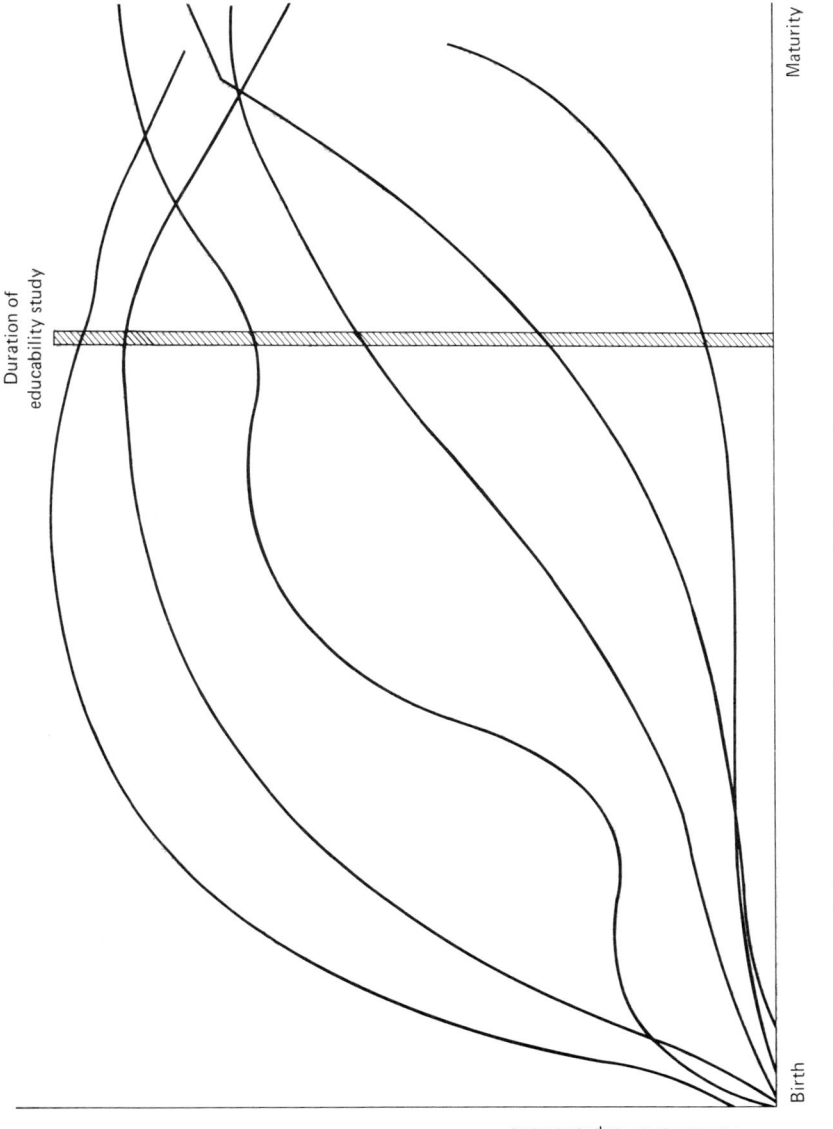

Figure 3.6 *Motor skill curves within a developmental framework.*

ple, one may simply subtract the first score obtained from the final level of performance reached within a number of trials. Other formulas involve computing the average improvement per trial, that is, dividing the total improvement by the number of trials which the individual has experienced; still other formulas discount improvement during the first trials as attributable to some kind of general warm-up effect, and measure learning by subtracting the performance levels at about trial three from the final ability scores posted.

Other formulas deal with the degree to which an individual has reached some hypothesized limit of learning. For example, if the task involves making fifteen out of fifteen free throws without a miss, ten free throws out of fifteen suggests that the individual has acquired 66.7 percent of the skill, based on the criterion of a perfect score.

One of the more valid means of evaluating skill learning involves computing the percentage of possible gain by using one of the following formulas:

1. $\dfrac{\text{sum of highest successive trials minus sum of first trials}}{\text{highest possible score minus sum of lowest scores}}$
2. $\dfrac{\text{sum of highest trials minus sum of first trials}}{\text{highest possible score minus sum of first trials}}$
3. $\dfrac{\text{sum of all trials minus sum of first trials}}{\text{highest possible score minus sum of first trials}}$

These formulas do not unnecessarily penalize individuals who start with high initial scores as contrasted to those who have low initial scores, as do some of the initial formulas outlined. Thus, with these "percentage of possible gain" formulas, more valid and equitable comparisons may be made among numerous individuals in a class exposed to a given skill, some of whom evidence high initial score and others of whom evidence relatively little previous exposure to the task at hand.

SUMMARY

The acquisition of motor skills involves a number of interrelated processes, some of which are readily measurable and some of which are not. Successive performance changes, not always indicative of true learning, are easily obtainable; when averaged by trial or plotted individually they result in what is termed a *performance curve.* Performance curves for individuals or groups take a number of forms indicative of early versus late improvement within a series of trials, of periods of little or no improvement (plateaus), or even of retrogression in performance, indicative of the influence of boredom, fatigue, and lack of motivation.

Motor skill acquisition involves not only selecting and smoothing movements and submovements into coherent sequences, but also selecting out relevant stimuli present within the performance situation. Moreover, at the higher skill levels, relatively subtle changes in visual-motor integration, respiration, and neural integration sometimes push final performance to levels higher than might be reasonably expected.

Skills tests composed of various balance and agility items have not generally been found to indicate any general motor educability factor. Instead, improvement in motor skills seems specific to each task, with relatively little transfer occurring from task to task within the time period of the experiments.

The measurement of motor skill improvement must take into account initial levels of performance, possible warm-up effects during initial trials, and the highest possible skill levels attainable for the task at hand. If these factors are not taken into account, those who initially perform well on a skill might be unduly penalized when their absolute improvement or rate of improvement is contrasted with those who perform poorly during the initial trials.

DISCUSSION QUESTIONS AND EXERCISES

1. On a piece of graph paper, plot your successive performance scores as you try to juggle two tennis balls using one hand (alternately throwing one at a time into the air).
2. Discuss the shape of your performance curve, with emphasis on the identification of the stages of learning and skill acquisition.
3. What might be learned as a single performance trial dips lower, as contrasted to the more successful trials coming before and after it?
4. Discuss the differences between learning and performance.
5. Devise a novel skill. Work out a scoring system. Try to determine what kind of acquisition curve you might obtain, before trying it yourself or on another student.
6. Using a target-throwing task, plot a learning curve and then, using the formulas given in the chapter, compute your learning score in various ways. Contrast the scores obtained. Which score do you consider the most valid measure of learning?
7. What are errors of commission and errors of omission? Give examples.
8. If a learning curve is mathematically extended (without actually recording more trials), what two kinds of information may be obtained?

9. What may cause plateaus in motor learning curves? What might be done to get a student off this type of plateau?
10. What are the implications of the "normal performance curve" in Figure 3.2(a) for the teaching of sports skills?
11. What is motor educability? What factors might contribute to the validity of this concept for a given individual?

BIBLIOGRAPHY

CONNOLLY, KEVIN, "Skill Development: Problems and Plans," Chapter 1 in *Mechanisms of Motor Skill Development*. New York: Academic Press, Inc., 1970.

CRATTY, BRYANT J., "Perceptual-Motor Learning, Based Upon Performance Measures," Chapter 16 in *Movement Behavior and Motor Learning* (2nd ed.). Philadelphia: Lea & Febiger, 1967.

———, "Learning to Execute a Perceptual-Motor Skill," Chapter 12 in *Psychology and Physical Activity*. Englewood Cliffs, N.J.: Prentice-Hall, Inc., 1968.

KNAPP, B., "Skill Defined," Chapter 1 in *Skill in Sport*. London: Routledge & Kegan Paul, 1964.

LAWTHER, JOHN D., "Methods in Early Stages of Skill-Learning," and "Motor Learning at Advanced Skill Levels," Chapters 4 and 5 in *The Learning of Physical Skills*. Englewood Cliffs, N.J.: Prentice-Hall, Inc., 1968.

NOBLE, CLYDE E., "Selective Learning," Chapter 2 in Edward A. Bilodeau, ed., *Acquisition of Skill*. New York: Academic Press, Inc., 1966.

OXENDINE, JOSEPH B., "General Learning Theory," Part 1 in *Psychology of Motor Learning*. New York: Appleton-Century-Crofts, 1968.

SAGE, GEORGE H., "Acquisition of Motor Skills," Chapter 16 in *Introduction to Motor-Behavior: A Neuropsychological Approach*. Reading, Mass.: Addison-Wesley Publishing Co., Inc., 1971.

SINGER, ROBERT N., "Basic Considerations in Motor Learning and Performance," Chapter 3 in *Motor Learning and Human Performance: An Application to Physical Education Skills*. New York: The Macmillan Company, 1968.

WHITING, H. T. A., "Introduction," Chapter 1 in *Acquiring Ball Skill, A Psychological Interpretation*. London: The Camelot Press Ltd., 1969.

4

Instructions

One of the most important aspects of motor skill learning is the use of instruction. Instructions have many dimensions and can be located on several scales. For example:

1. Some instructions are given to a performer by himself, while others come from an observing teacher or coach.
2. Instructions may be given at various time periods relative to task performance. Thus, instructions are given before practice of the task, during the execution of a task, and/or following performance.
3. Instructions may be general in nature ("see if you can move more accurately"), or very specific ("Now try to lift your arm higher during the stroke recovery").
4. Instructions may be intended to motivate, or may be designed to inform the performer of his relative success or failure as compared to some standard.
5. Instructions may be designed to be transmitted through one or through some combination of sensory modalities. For example, consider the influence of visual demonstration, verbal description, and manual guidance as aids in teaching individuals to execute a motor skill.
6. Another important consideration is who (instructor or student) is permitted to make what instructional and curricular decisions about what phases of the program.

7. A final dimension of instructions concerns whether the learner is engaging in trial-and-error practice or whether his efforts are carefully guided. A subproblem within this general area concerns whether the trials are thought out without accompanying actions, or whether actions accompany the trials.

In this chapter, particular emphasis will be placed upon the interaction of self-instructions and formally extended instructions, the placement of instructions in time, the use of various sensory modalities within the instructional process, and the manner in which instructional decisions may be shifted from teacher to learner. Overall, the intent is to illustrate how the teacher should try to account for individual differences in the students he or she is attempting to reach. An effort is also made to illustrate how the most effective teachers may be those who are flexible in their approach to the teaching of motor skills. Indeed, I believe that one of the more important axioms to be derived from scrutiny of the literature on skill learning is the realization by the instructor that "everyone does not learn as I do."

Learners Talk to Themselves!

The earliest studies of motor skill frequently were the result of the interactions between one professor and a single student. Sitting opposite each other at a table, they might alternately attempt a skill; in their write-up they would describe the thoughts that went through their minds while working on the task and the strategies they adopted or rejected as they tried to improve their performances.

Although such research quickly became scientifically unrespectable because of the subjective nature of the reports obtained, within recent years the same type of data has been used again to describe what people think while they learn skills. More recent studies have employed tape recorders and videotape machines to combine what the performer thinks about, or says he is thinking about, with the actual motions he makes. The results of these investigations are the following principles relative to self-instruction:

1. There are wide individual differences in the quantity and quality of instructions an individual gives himself as he practices a motor skill.
2. Different elements are concentrated on different stages in skill acquisition.
3. Most of the time a learner is concentrating on only a single component of the complex skill he is attempting to acquire.
4. Finally, the quantity of self-instruction generally diminishes as skill is acquired unless plateaus are reached in the learning process, which evidence a block that proves frustrating to the learner.

Perhaps the most important finding is the third. The learner somehow knows that he may attend only to a single component to make one correction at a time as he attempts a motor skill. He does not usually overload himself. Several inferences may be derived from this important observation:

1. Anyone attempting to offer instructions to the learner should probably try to discover which component of the skill seems important for the learner to attend to at a given moment in the learning process.
2. The instructor should try not to overload the learner with strategies which are incompatible with what he may be attempting to accomplish himself via self-instruction.
3. Attempts should be made to find out what the learner feels is important about a skill so that the more experienced instructor may weigh the importance of the element and at times change the direction of the instructions the learner may be giving himself.
4. The instructor should, by asking the learner, determine in what terms the learner is attempting to translate skill components to himself so that the same terms may be employed by the instructor. In this manner, a great deal of the redundancy which often accompanies the verbal interactions of coach (instructor) and learner may be reduced or even eliminated.
5. The instructor, with his theoretically better background, should be able to offer the learner the best advice necessary, relative to skill mechanics, so that qualitative self-instruction may take place.
6. The teacher or coach should determine what elements occupy the learner's attention before interjecting his comments and instructional efforts.

A model depicting the interaction of self-instructions with those imposed from sources outside the learner is shown in Figure 4.1. In general, the instructor should attempt to determine the nature, type, and timing of the learner's self-instruction, and then in a compatible and helpful way he should insert his instructions into the consciousness of the learner.

INSTRUCTIONS IN TIME

Instructions from persons other than the learner may be given at various times in relation to the performance of the task itself. For example, instructions may be offered before the first trial of a task, while performance is taking place, between trials, at the completion of a trial, or after several trials. Usually instructions after several trials are labeled "knowledge of results" or "information feedback."

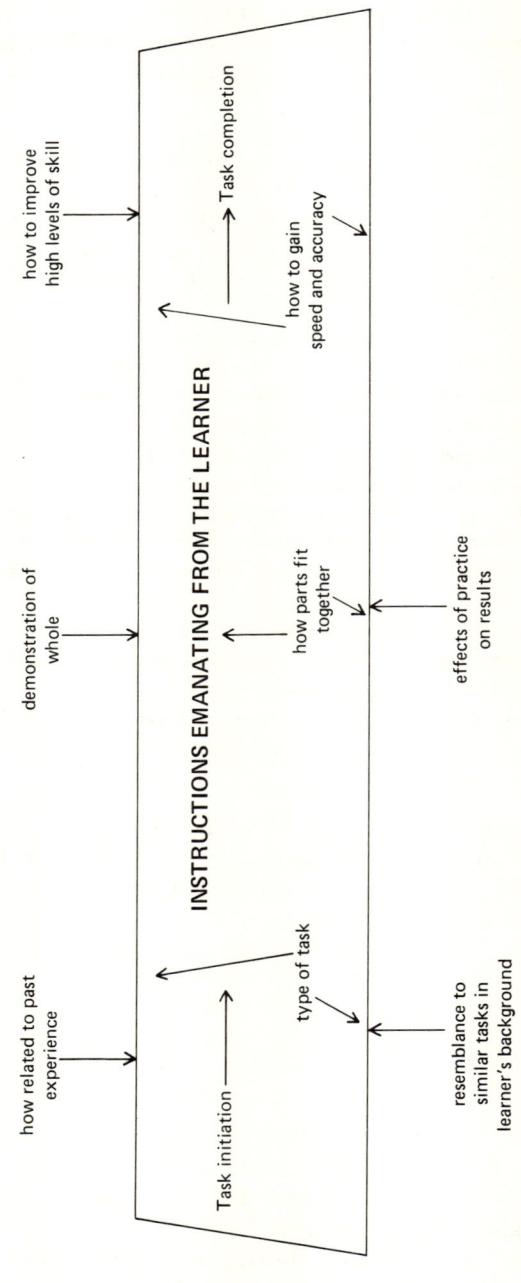

Figure 4.1 *Interactions of various types of instructions during the learning of a motor skill.*

In general, research holds that the quality and quantity of helpful instructions often differ at various times within the learning process. Certain types of instructions are usually more appropriate before practice, while other types are often more instructive during the middle or latter stages of skill acquisition.

Analyses of the qualities which contribute to progressive improvement of skills indicate that instruction given before the task should be fairly detailed and should concern the spatial dimensions of the movements, the mechanical principles involved, and/or the strategies which might be employed during the learning process. For example, instruction might concern whether it would be better to break the task into parts or to deal with it as a whole. Research has indicated that mentally retarded children may learn to execute reasonably complex skills almost as well as normal children if enough pertinent preperformance instruction is offered to them.

However, if the impending task involves great stress, particularly if it involves participating on a competitive athletic team within view of many spectators, it is usually considered unsound to confront the performer with a great deal of technical information just before the game or contest. Instead, thorough preperformance training should have been given in the days and months before the contest, rather than immediately before it, under stress.

Information from several sources reaches the performer as he moves through the task. Thus, care should be taken to give the performer a minimum amount of information while he is performing and during the brief pauses between trials. Research indicates that, particularly after the learner has discovered the similarity between the task he is engaged in and previous ones, and after an initial "discovery stage" has passed, information concerning correction of the movements themselves should be offered. For example, directions might include "move faster" or "keep your arm higher on the stroke recovery."

Information offered following the completion of a task or a performance trial is usually referred to as "knowledge of results" or "information feedback." During this period pertinent information concerning the performer's relative success at meeting his goal or the degree to which his movement pattern conformed to some hypothesized ideal may be extended. In general, research indicates that information feedback should be governed by several pertinent principles:

1. The knowledge should be specific, clearly presented, and frequent; that is, it should be given after every one or two trials.
2. The information should be offered in terms the learner can understand. For example, while college sprinters might be shown time-force graphs

of their efforts, small children should be given less sophisticated evidence of their relative success.
3. The information should be offered in several forms, verbally, through some kind of moving picture (videotape or the like), as well as through a demonstration.
4. Care should be taken to show the learner what he did wrong—the type of errors he committed—as well as what were the correct components within his efforts.
5. If information concerning performance is given too soon after a trial, it may be confusing. Research indicates that a small time lapse before giving knowledge of results should be allowed to let the feel of the movement somehow "set" in the performer's consciousness.
6. Finally, specific rather than more general information is usually more helpful. Exact corrections concerning running style, pitching form, and so on are more meaningful and more likely to produce rapid improvement on the part of the learner than are general directions to "try harder," "put more force into it," and the like.

SENSORY CHANNEL

Directions accompanying attempts at motor skill development may be arranged so that they affect predominantly one or several sense organs. They may be presented visually or verbally, or the performer may be asked to perform and "feel" the movement. Similarly, he may be guided through the movement by the instructor's manipulating the body parts involved.

Available research points to several general and specific guidelines governing optimum use of the various ways of presenting information while individuals attempt to improve themselves in physical skills. For example, it is generally found that instructional methods which combine several approaches to transmitting information are more effective than approaches in which only one method is employed. As learners seem to acquire information in highly individualistic ways, it seems important for an instructor to be adroit at presenting information in several forms. Specific guidelines for transmitting information compatible with specific sensory channels are outlined below.

Instructions through Vision

Instructions involving visual input may be presented to the learner in several ways, including a demonstration by the instructor or a fellow class member, a demonstration film showing an expert performing the task, or by either a videotape or a film of the learner himself performing a task for one or more trials.

When a demonstrator is employed, it is important that two considerations be kept in mind. The observers must identify with the demonstrator and feel that they are like him at least in some way and have a reasonable chance to imitate his movements; second, the observer must be able to understand and remember the often complex sequences of movement required in some tasks.

For a demonstration to be effective, it is sometimes useful to employ a class member, an average performer with whom the other class members may identify. Often demonstrations by experts, in person or on film, are less than effective because the class members cannot imagine themselves ever being as good as the demonstrator they are encouraged to copy. At the same time, the less than adroit demonstrator may unwillingly make common mistakes, which, when pointed out, might make subsequent learning by the other class members more effective.

On the other hand, a visual demonstration, if too inept, may not be a sufficient model for imitation. Observing a series of incorrect subactions within a complex task may be less than helpful. Thus, high-level performers in particular require a high-level demonstration in person or on film.

The same dichotomy between experts and beginning performers should be kept in mind when immediate visual feedback via videotaped performance is employed as a means of enhancing motor skill. Videotape of one's performance may be extremely helpful for several reasons. There is less ambiguity in instructor–student communication when the visual presentation of a complex performance task is seen by both than when the same performance is discussed verbally between the two parties. The performer *has* to believe what he sees, while he may not believe or interpret clearly verbal communications emanating from his coach or physical education instructor.

While the expert may be aided by viewing his performance, the less adroit may be somewhat disturbed by receiving clear and irrefutable evidence of his ineptitude via videotape. Studies of beginning dancers who could watch themselves from the rear while moving for the first time, and of beginning gymnasts who likewise saw their crude attempts on videotape, have shown that beginners must not be exposed too soon to such concrete evidence of how they look when performing.

Several other guidelines should be followed when you are employing filmed, videotaped, or live demonstrations of complex sports skills:

    1. To analyze the rapid movements occurring in many performance acts such as baseball pitching, several technical requirements should be adhered to (the use of rapid film, at least one hundred frames a second;

the performance filmed from many angles; and so on). Following the film a well-qualified scholar familiar with biomechanical analysis of motor activities should be on hand to aid correct interpretation of the film. Interpretation of a filmed motor act is only as good as the background of those carrying out the analysis; if no qualified individual is available, the filming session is often a waste of time and money.

2. Filmed or videotaped efforts enabling self-inspection by the performer are probably more beneficial in some activities than in others. For example, these techniques are most helpful in those activities in which the visual field of the performer undergoes distortion while performing (tumbling, trampolining, and gymnastic activities; selected track and field events including pole vaulting and high jumping).

3. The immediacy of the visual knowledge of performance is important; videotape feedback immediately after each pole vault, for example, if correctly analyzed, is considerably more helpful than if the performer obtains information about his performance only after the film has been processed, several days later.

4. Filmed analyses are helpful in team sports in the study of the movements of several players at one time. No coach can be expected, when viewing his basketball team, to remember in detail what each player did during each play or portion of the game. However, the manner in which such a team-film is employed is important. If the film sessions after football games are treated by coaches as a "club" to punish less able players; the knowledge that this may transpire may add additional stress to the players during the game and impede rather than enhance their efforts.

To aid motor skill learning, visual information via film or demonstrations should be presented so that it is easily understood by the performer and should be accompanied by expert interpretation. Visual aids should be presented between performance trials if possible, or at least immediately after performance trials. Under some circumstances, as with possibly self-conscious beginners, too vivid a portrayal of ineptitude via film or videotape may prove disturbing. Live demonstrations should be easily perceived, organized, and remembered by those viewing them; the viewers should be able to identify with the demonstrator, perceiving similarities between themselves and the skill level, sex, and/or age of the performer.

Verbal Instructions

In general, the limited research on the topic holds that most extensive verbal instruction should be offered before or during the initial stages of learning a motor skill. Verbal instructions should be given when the individual is not attempting to concentrate single-mindedly on his self-instructions. They should be given *between* performance trials rather than during the performance.

Verbal instructions should be understandable to the learners, but if possible they should be gauged to test his upper limits of understanding. A college physics major on the gymnastic team should be instructed, between attempts to execute a complicated stunt on the high-bar, in terms of the physics and mechanics of the actions, rather than in the general terms appropriate for the high school gymnast.

Individual differences in intelligence among team performers should be considered when the coach is communicating verbally about sports skills or tactics. Care should be taken not to talk down to bright or average youngsters or to talk above the youths who may be less capable intellectually. Either mistake is self-defeating.

Most successful verbal directions, particularly those given during the later stages of learning and those directed toward high-level athletes, are very specific in regard to corrections and improvements of tactics and skills, and at the same time are held to a minimum. The advanced performer wants to perform, not to listen to lectures unless they are short and pertinent to his performance needs. Overly verbal coaches are oppressive to many athletes.

Perhaps the most important ingredient in successful instruction and coaching of physical skills is a thorough knowledge of all the parameters of the sport one is coaching. I recently had the pleasure of conversing with one of the most successful college swimming coaches in the country. His knowledge of people and of swimming was profound, but equally deep was his background in fluid hydraulics and in the physiology of exercise. Yet this coach pointed out that he usually withheld much of his scientific knowledge from his swimmers; indeed, he felt that most of it was usually unnecessary and could even confuse the swimmers. However, the possession of this background makes his answers to their questions broad and deep, a condition which earns him a great deal of respect among his athletes and which enables him to perceive the "whys" of the training regimes he imposes.

Verbal information, like visual information, should be judiciously inserted within the practice schedule, should be pertinent and specific to the task, and should not be pedagogically oppressive to the athlete. The quality of verbal instructions is directly related to the thorough knowledge of the instructor in relation to the sport or physical activity.

Instructions through Movement

Movement instructions may be given in two ways. The instructor may permit physical practice by the learner, unencumbered by any kind of manual guidance; or he may attempt to manipulate the limbs and/or the total body of the performer, by grasping him with or without the use of ancillary devices or equipment.

Research has shown that some individuals seem to learn best via movement rather than through visual or verbal directions. Movement-oriented individuals may cause some instructors consternation if they stop listening to him or watching a demonstration in favor of practicing on their own to "feel" the movements they have been briefly exposed to via other modalities.

There are indications that young children often learn well when their limbs are manipulated through a movement. Children who possess visual-perceptual handicaps are often taught well by this means, as they lack the capacities to organize and remember a complex visual demonstration, and to unconsciously "catch" the movements of their peers in culturally accepted sports skills and even in basic movements like running, throwing, jumping, and landing. Data from the limited research on this topic illuminate several principles in the use of manual guidance in the teaching of learning and retention of motor skills:

1. When offering manual guidance of physical skills, the instructor should position himself so that he has the same visual frame of reference as the learner. For example, when instructing manual skills at a desk, the instructor should guide the hands of the learner by standing behind him, rather than by facing the learner across the desk and requiring the performer not only to imitate but also to reverse the movements to which he is exposed. In one study learning was 30 to 40 percent more effective when this rule was followed.

2. Movements should not be overguided by the instructor. That is, even if his limbs are being grasped in some way, the performer should be able to control himself through as much of the movement as possible. Moreover, the manual guidance should be phased out as quickly as possible, permitting the learner to take over control as soon as his abilities permit. The findings from one study point out that manual guidance, while aiding immediate performance improvement, was not as helpful as expected in the retention of skill. It seems that overguiding a movement may result, as the performer at times "fights" the guidance, in somehow programming in to the performer a motor pattern incompatible with the precise movement to be acquired.

WHOSE INSTRUCTIONS ARE IMPORTANT?

One important practical and philosophical consideration in the use of instructions is who should make decisions about what, in settings in which an obvious leader-coach-teacher has been designated. Resolution of this question is not easy and must take into consideration operational, situational, and social components within the learning environment.

It seems obvious to some that for any kind of change in motor behavior (learning) to take place, some kind of instruction is needed. That is, there must be a designated place, a reasonably coherent group of activities should transpire, and someone or some group should make the various decisions which apparently need to be made about what should be practiced. How often practice should occur, what means should be employed to achieve the end results, and what the end result should be seem to be additional necessary decisions.

Philosophical questions which must be answered before the above problems may be resolved include whether we view physical activities and movement skills as ends in themselves, or as a vehicle for personal, social, intellectual, and/or emotional change. If we believe that the final product of instructional procedures is superior performance, instructional decisions will probably be largely retained by the teacher-coach. It is usually obvious, at least to him, that he knows most about the intricacies of the skill or sport; thus, he is usually rather direct in his effort to inform, to instruct, and to teach the action patterns he desires in his team or class.

On the other hand, if physical activities are viewed as a means not only to the enhancement of movement attributes, but also to a modification of the individual's personality in other ways, different strategies are desirable. For example, it is suggested that more flexible movement behaviors and more personal change will be elicited in performance situations if the learners have opportunities to make decisions about how practice is conducted, about the content of a lesson, about the extent to which goals are to be reached, and even about the objectives to be attained.

From a practical and a theoretical standpoint, coaches and physical educators have suggested and carried out various kinds of teaching and coaching strategies intended to give the learner more decisions within the instructional process. For example, at least one coach has permitted his players before each game, to select democratically the makeup of the starting team.

One methodologist has recommended that decisions about the learning environment be transferred to the learner, when and if he is ready to take them, with decisions about task modifications being transferred first (where, when to start, how many, and so on). If this is successful, decisions about evaluation can be transferred to the learner, that is, learners work in pairs or small groups and evaluate each other's performances. Finally, if these strategies seem successful and some learning-structure is maintained, decisions about what is to go into a lesson may be given to the learners. Students may, with some basic information, devise lessons which meet their individual needs to "get strong," to "learn to play ball," and so on. Such a teaching strategy may have several operational outcomes, although research data are extremely rare and prediction difficult:

1. There is more work for the teacher in deciding when to transfer decisions about what to whom. The teacher also has a responsibility to know a great deal about the movements and sports skills involved in the lesson.
2. Decision transfer is often emotionally disturbing to both the learners and the teacher, who have been accustomed to highly structured programs.
3. Decision transfer may be attempted only by instructors whose needs for order and control of their environment are not too pronounced.
4. Sports skills are often learned best under conditions in which the instructor makes most of the decisions, while flexibility in tactics often develop to a higher degree in situations in which the participants have been asked to discover principles which govern the course of the game and the acquisition of skill.
5. More vigorous physical participation is often forthcoming under conditions in which learners have had an opportunity to construct and/or to modify their lesson's content.
6. More meaningful intellectual participation occurs in environments in which the learners perceive a real opportunity to take part in planning the nature and direction of their subsequent efforts.

In general, the strategy of shifting decisions to the learners, while fraught with intellectual and emotional peril for some instructors and coaches, is potentially an expansive and meaningful experience for the learners. At the same time, both instructors and their charges must come to terms with such questions as their basic goals in physical activity situations, the amount of structure they perceive as needed, and their needs for controlling others.

SUMMARY

Information of various kinds, in several forms, and at various speeds reaches the individual performing a motor skill. Continuous information is obtained as the feel of the movement is perceived, while discontinuous information arrives via various signs that he is achieving some kind of relative success (the ball striking or failing to strike the target), as well as in the form of instructions and directions from the observing teacher or coach.

Research over the past seventy years has indicated that people give themselves vocal instructions as they perform; their instructions may or may not coincide with those offered by the instructor. Usually self-instructions zero in on a single specific subskill or strategy within a given time dimension. Thus, the job of the instructor is often to complement these self-instructions or at least to interfere with them as little as possible as the skill is being acquired.

Overall, research suggests that effective instruction of motor skills is pertinent, compatible with the needs of the learner and the level of learning of the performer, and available through several sensory channels such as verbal instruction, visual demonstration, the opportunity for practice, and/or manual guidance of some kind. Information from an outside source should not overload the learner's ability to monitor and comprehend information which is usually arriving or available from several sources at the same time.

Finally, there are philosophical decisions which the instructor needs to make, relating to the degree to which trial-and-error practice versus carefully instructed practice is demanded by the learner and to how many decisions of what type should be made by the learner versus the instructor-coach within the total learning environment.

DISCUSSION QUESTIONS AND EXERCISES

1. What kinds of instruction are most effective before practice, during practice, after practice?
2. Contrast the possible interfering versus facilitating effects of instructor instructions versus performer self-instructions.
3. Discuss the manner in which knowledge of results might be made most helpful to the learner.
4. How might a visual demonstration be made most effective?
5. In what ways might you make instructions least effective?
6. Form teams of three: performer, observer, instructor. Select either a familiar or a novel skill to be taught to the performer. Assume that the performer has had no previous exposure to the skill. The instructor should attempt to teach the skill. The observer should analyze how the instructor could have been more or less effective. Let the performer reveal how the instructions confused or aided him. Write down the performer's self-instructions.
7. Discuss the possible advantages and drawbacks of immediate videotape feedback of successive performance efforts. What factors would contribute to or detract from efficient learning under these conditions?

8. Discuss the interaction of verbal instructions with videotape feedback of performance.
9. Discuss the advantages and disadvantages of manual guidance of a motor skill.
10. Discuss the manner in which skill difficulty, skill type, and intellectual competences of the learner influence the nature and type of instructions offered.

BIBLIOGRAPHY

CRATTY, BRYANT J., "Instruction," Chapter 4 in *Movement Behavior and Motor Learning*. Philadelphia: Lea & Febiger, 1967.

KNAPP, B., "Factors Affecting the Acquisition of Skill," Chapter 4 in *Skill in Sport*. London: Routledge & Kegan Paul, 1963.

SAGE, GEORGE H., "The Special Senses: The Eyes," Chapter 7 in *Introduction to Motor Behavior: A Neuropsychological Approach*. Reading, Mass.: Addison-Wesley Publishing Co., Inc., 1971.

SINGER, ROBERT N., "Teaching Methodology," Chapter 7 in *Motor Learning and Human Performance*. New York: The Macmillan Company, 1968.

WHITING, H. T. A., "Acquiring Skill in Ball Games," Chapter 6 in *Acquiring Ball Skill*. London: G. Bell & Sons Ltd., 1969.

5

Quantitative, Qualitative, and Temporal Aspects of Motor Skill Practice

A group of factors which have been found to exert important influence on the speed with which people learn skills includes the manner in which practice sessions and trials are spaced in time, and how much of the total skill is practiced at one time.

A great deal of research is available on the influence of massing versus spacing motor skill practice in time. However, there are few viable theoretical models by which the findings may be explained and organized, taking into consideration such variables as the duration of the practice, the duration and frequency of the trials, and the nature of the motor task.

We have less information about the influence on performance and learning of practicing parts versus practicing the whole of a complex motor task. The guidelines pertaining to whole versus part practice are therefore more inferential than absolute.

Despite the limitations outlined above, how skills are practiced within a time dimension and whole versus part practice are important factors to consider when studying the teaching of motor skills. While sometimes limited by curriculum considerations, teachers usually retain the perogative of either exposing their charges to several trials of a given skill within a narrow time span, or giving them trials spaced throughout single lessons distributed during a week or throughout a school semester. Teachers of physical activity often may also determine whether their students should learn parts of a task before attempting the skill in its entirety, or whether the total skill will be presented at once.

MASSING AND DISTRIBUTING PRACTICE IN TIME

The first researchers who dealt with the memorization of nonsense syllables quickly became interested in the influence of spacing practice trials in time on performance levels achieved and retention. The same facet of practice was similarly explored by those who researched motor skill acquisition.

Later scholars were at first surprised to find in their data a phenomenon not usually seen by those investigating verbal skills. It appeared that, at times, spacing trials of motor skill practice had a positive effect on learning and on final performance levels reached over a given number of practices. During the years that followed, the effect of spacing practice on motor skill improvement attracted the attention of numerous scholars.[1]

The Variety of Practice Schedules

In research studies and in life, an almost unlimited number of combinations of massed versus distributed practice schedules are possible. For example, trials may be massed with short time intervals between each in a uniform schedule, or an even schedule of practice trials spaced with

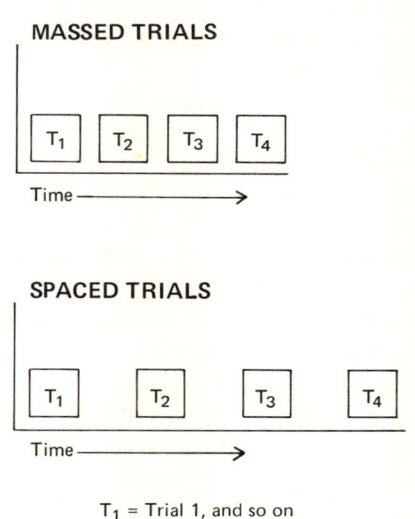

Figure 5.1

---

[1] Some of them, even though employing motor skills as experimental tasks, purported to be evaluating mental growth and similar intellectual qualities.

a relatively long time interval between each trial may be adopted. These two possibilities are diagrammed in Figure 5.1.

The trials may be initially massed and then gradually spaced in time, as in Figure 5.2.

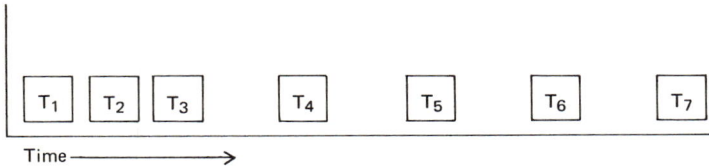

Figure 5.2

Conversely, trials may be initially spaced and then gradually brought closer together, as in Figure 5.3.

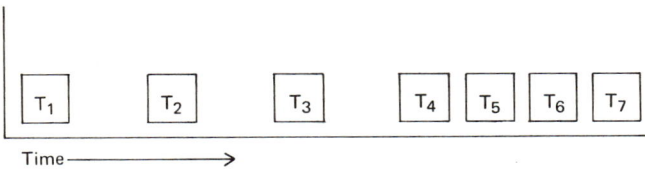

Figure 5.3

Practice may be regularly spaced in time, and then at various times, groups of massed practice trials may be interpolated into the practice schedule, as in Figure 5.4.

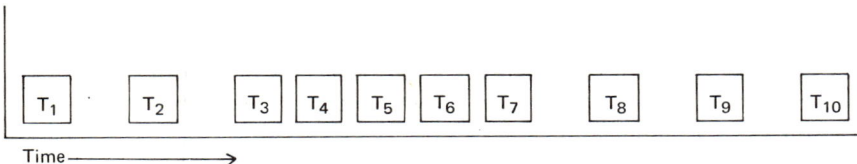

Figure 5.4

Or the converse may occur; that is, trials may be massed in time, and then at various points groups of trials with longer time periods between trials may be inserted, as in Figure 5.5.

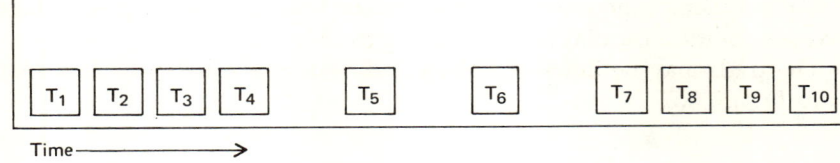

Figure 5.5

Trials may be spaced, massed, or subject to one of the other conditions diagrammed above, within a *single* continuous practice session, and/or practice *sessions* may be arranged in time so that they correspond to some of the above conditions, as in Figure 5.6.

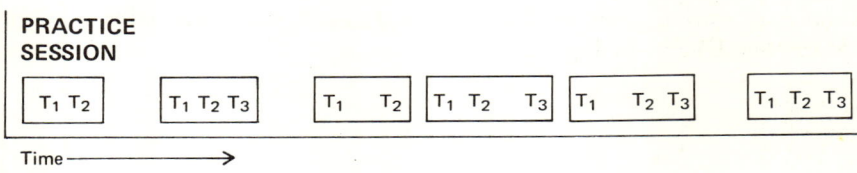

Figure 5.6

Two or more of the combinations may be incorporated into a series of practice trials, affording even further variety.

Effects of Timing on Performance Levels

Although much of the literature indicates that motor skill learning and performance is facilitated if practice trials are spaced rather than massed in time, this generalization does not always hold. For example, if an individual is highly motivated and resistant to the boredom or inhibition which often builds up when rather simple tasks are practiced incessantly, massed practice will probably elicit higher levels of learning from him more quickly. That quick learning is occurring may motivate him further and elicit even more effort from him.

Other research has found that the performance of retarded children is sometimes not negatively influenced if trials are massed closely together in time. This has been explained by suggesting that retardates may not become as quickly bored, and thus do not evidence the task inhibition that is apparent when the normal child is exposed to the same practice conditions.

In general, however, spacing facilitates performance improvement, particularly when plateaus, periods of little or no improvement, are recorded when successive performance efforts are plotted.

As practice on a task progresses, two psychological phenomena are mutually interacting, one to blunt performance, and the second to facilitate improvement. It is axiomatic that practicing a task at least initially elicits improvement as various obvious and subtle learning processes take place. However, as practice progresses a negative psychological force termed *inhibition* also begins to build up: boredom and/or aversion or resistance to the task. Inhibition may be particularly marked when the ratio between the ability of the learner and the difficulty of the task reaches certain relationships. For example, the most marked inhibition due to massing practice will occur when:

1. The learner is capable and intelligent, and the task is simple and/or similar to those which the learner has experienced before.[2]
2. The learner is not very capable, and the task is perceived by him as complex.

Moderate amounts of inhibition will occur when:

3. The learner is moderately capable, and the task is of moderate difficulty.
4. The learner is not very capable and/or intelligent, and the task is extremely simple.

Little inhibition will occur when:

5. The task is reasonably complex, and the capable learner perceives it as a challenge.

The general guidelines must be modified as learning progresses. That is, a task may initially seem complex and thus challenging to a learner, but after he begins to master it, it becomes less interesting and inhibition builds up. Under these conditions, initially massing practice will probably produce the best and quickest improvement, while during the later stages of learning, trials should be spaced to dissipate some of the inhibition which may build up.

Similarly, a retarded youngster may find a task initially too complex, but on being led toward its execution, he may begin to find it challenging; thus, he may be initially facilitated by spacing practice and then stimulated more by gradually or suddenly massing practice.

[2] Indeed, under these conditions capable individuals often create complexity in tasks by introducing their own modifications and thus attempting to reduce the inhibition and aversion toward the task which they begin to perceive in themselves.

Recently, sophisticated scholars have taken a closer look at some of the critical variables within the question of the temporal order of practice sessions. They have, for example, begun to examine the ratios of the duration of practice sessions to the length of rest periods between tasks. These work–rest ratios, it seems, are more important influences on improvement than is the duration of the rest periods themselves.

A work–rest ratio of one to one means that the duration of the practice period is equal to the time between practices. A ratio of two to one means that the practice time is twice that of the rest period; one to three means that the rest period is three times as long as the practice session.

In general, for the most efficient practice, when the practice session is long, the following rest period should be of similar duration, either equal to or longer than the practice period, depending on the task. The work–rest ratio needs adjusting in one direction—more rest to less work time—when the task is either physically and/or psychologically taxing, while if the task is pleasant to the learner and not taxing or oppressive, the work–rest ratio may be adjusted in the opposite direction.

Why Spacing Practice Sometimes Helps

Several theories have been advanced to explain why motor skill seems to improve markedly if practice trials are spaced in time.[3] The concept of response inhibition is used by at least one theoretician to explain the positive performance effects of permitting time to elapse between practice efforts. That is, while practice elicits improvement, the performer's inhibition toward the task may be given an opportunity to dissipate if time periods are introduced between trials. Plateaus due to task aversion may be outdistanced if practice which may formerly have been massed is distributed in time. Negatively accelerated performance curves may change to positively accelerated performance patterns with the introduction of rest intervals of increasing duration.

A "neural reverberation" theory has also been advanced to explain why improvement in motor skills sometimes occurs with no physical practice. It is supposed that when a skill is first practiced, the motor pattern is faintly traced within the nervous system; when rest occurs, the random electric activity that is a constant characteristic of the nervous system somehow more thoroughly entrenches the neural pattern supporting the skill. Thus, when reperformance occurs, the act is performed at a higher

---

[3] Thus, when spacing practice elicits more improvement than massing practice in time, the axiom "practice makes perfect" might better be stated, "no practice may elicit more improvement than does practice!"

level because of the effects of a kind of electric etching process within the nervous system.

Other more prosaic theories suggest that during rest, selective conscious and unconscious remembering and forgetting occur. That is, during the rest between trials, there is a selective forgetting of inappropriate responses and subresponses, while the appropriate components of the tasks are retained, remembered, and reflected in subsequent performance efforts.

Whatever the cause, the teacher should take advantage of the spontaneous improvement often seen when practice is spaced. The learner seems to need time for the skill to "settle" within his neural mechanisms and his consciousness. Practice which is demanding, oppressive, and repeated at short intervals often has a depressing effect on performance levels.

WHOLE VERSUS PART PRACTICE

Although the research on whole versus part practice is not as extensive as that dealing with massing versus spacing of practice, some guidelines exist which may be helpful to the fledgling instructor of physical skills. Again, a number of subjective and flexible scales should be taken into consideration as we approach this second topic. For example, how much of a component constitutes what might be termed a "whole" for a given individual? How may subskills be grouped so that they become manageable units for a group of learners to ingest? Skills with discrete and separate response components can be broken into parts; others, more continuous in nature, are more likely to be viewed and practiced as a whole. Let us consider the principles underlying whole versus part practice rather than searching for the exact formula, as the numerous dimensions of the topic complicate the assignment of precise laws.

Progressive-Part Practice

In most situations "pure" part practice is not carried on; it is obviously so inefficient to practice separately the parts of a task before putting them together that what is termed *progressive-part practice* is used instead. In other words, the individual practices the first part of a skill (tossing up the tennis ball) and then a second part (bringing the racket back), and then puts both parts together before practicing a third part by itself (hitting the ball, following through, taking a step toward the net), which is then combined with the first two parts, and practiced as a whole.

Progressive-part practice of moderately complex skills has been shown to be helpful with retarded children, while for extremely complex skills, even normal youngsters may benefit from this approach.

Some tasks by their very nature require the learner to engage in part or progressive-part practice. For example, studies of the learning of typing and telegraphy skills usually reveal performance curves marked by several plateaus. Searching for the reasons behind the plateaus, several writers have suggested that initially the performers of both tasks learned to respond to single letter cues; that is, the typist learned the location of the individual letters on the keyboard, and when transcribing written material could only "think-and-type" one letter at a time. With increased practice the performers began to evidence what might be termed *word-responses;* for example, when the telegraph operators heard or read a word, their fingers moved to form a total word response without having to think through each word. This level of performance remained constant for a period of time until certain often-used phrases such as "sincerely yours" began to be translated into quick total-response patterns on typewriter and telegraph keys. Thus, the individuals moved from word to phrase responses, exceeding their final performance plateaus.

The process of building up increasingly complex response patterns from simpler ones should be put into operation when good instructors and efficient learners jointly approach the acquisition of complex skills in which larger muscle groups are operative. Both parties should attempt to determine what simple, easily acquired responses contribute to more global, complex ones. Practice should then proceed, gradually adding one response group to another, if the individual cannot acquire the total skill in a more broad manner.

Part and progressive-part practice is on the surface inefficient, but in many situations, with certain kinds of tasks and less capable performers, it may prove indispensable. Understanding thoroughly the skills one is attempting to transmit, particularly the basic components, is an important adjunct to effective teaching. What must be avoided, however, is the unfortunate tendency of many coaches and physical education teachers to break down or analyze to an absurd degree; the tendency sometimes leads to performer paralysis.

Whole Practice

Practicing the whole task, within the learner's capabilities, usually proves more motivating as quicker improvement is usually elicited. No time is needed to integrate the various parts with one another, as is the case when a skill is learned in parts. Moreover, when the whole task is presented to the performer, he is able to perceive and intellectually organize its totality, including the manner in which various components fit together. Comprehensive inspection of the task is not always possible when the part and progressive-part methods are employed.

Certain kinds of tasks seem to be most easily learned by the whole method, such as gymnastic skills which are fluid in nature like the kip or upstart on the high-bar, and swimming strokes. Aquatic skills, however, must be presented as parts when the performers are not mature, or are intellectually incapable of organizing the entire stroke.

Continuous skills are more easily learned by most performers by the whole method. On the other hand, complex tasks, particularly those involving pauses in time, are often best acquired by the progressive-part method.

SPEED VERSUS ACCURACY

Another qualitative difference in skill acquisition is whether the speed qualities of the skill level finally sought are demanded of the learner during the initial stages of skill acquisition or at a later stage. That is, when a rapid ballistic action is desired (a tennis serve or a baseball throw for distance), should the learner attempt to replicate the speed desired by the time of the final trials during his initial attempts at the task? Whether a performer attempts first to achieve accuracy and then to develop speed, or the reverse, probably depends to some degree on his basic approach to a number of tasks. Some individuals are risk-takers, who do not mind performing poorly but rapidly; others are more careful and prefer accuracy over speed during their initial confrontations with a motor task. The same individual differences are seen in instructors, some of whom prefer to emphasize speed initially, while others demand accuracy before attempting to mold the speed of the movements.

Some tasks require high rates of speed by their very nature, others demand less speed but more accuracy. While experimental literature does not contain a great number of studies concerning this question, some basic principles are suggested by the available information. For example:

1. From a neurological standpoint, a rapidly performed movement is very different from one performed slowly, even though both may require movement of the body and/or limbs through the same spatial dimensions. A very different kind of neuromotor "program" seems to be initiated in the cortex of the brain when the velocity of the same apparent movement is changed from slow to fast, or vice versa.
2. Hazardous activities, and those in which the visual field suffers disorientation from the upright (tumbling movements, for example), are

probably best learned with assistance which permits them to be performed somewhat slower than is finally desired. Indeed, primate mothers, when teaching their young to negotiate tree branches, are known to assist them through complex gymnastics, initially performed slowly.

3. A movement should be practiced at its final speed as soon as possible, without undue disruption of accuracy. As is true of use of whole practice, however, the instructor must determine at what speed a given learner may be expected to perform the skill without marked disruption of accuracy.[4]
4. Some parts of some movements may be practiced at full speed initially, while others may be practiced at partial speed until facility is acquired.
5. Initial practice at partial speed gives the individual an intellectual awareness of the spatial dimensions of the task and of the mechanical principles governing its performance. Some individuals may need initial slow practice, if they are more analytic in nature and need time to acquire a cognitive awareness of what they are doing; others will be more confused than aided by an initial slowing down of the movement and will prefer to practice rapidly during the initial trials.

Despite the blanket statement in some books that deal with the principles of motor learning and physical education that "initial rapid practice is best," the data supporting that contention are extremely limited and come from research in only a narrow range of motor tasks. In the absence of an extensive bibliography dealing with this specific topic, it is believed that the guidelines outlined above, if judiciously applied, should serve the teacher well.

SUMMARY

Overall, research into the parameters of motor skill acquisition seems to support the validity of the following principles:

1. Spaced practice often elicits higher performance levels when the task becomes physically taxing or psychologically oppressive to the learner.
2. Practice massed in time is best if the performer is highly motivated and the task proves complex enough to offer him a challenge, but not difficult enough to thwart his efforts.

[4] Indeed, detailed analysis of movements has begun to indicate that no apparently stereotyped movement is performed in exactly the same way by the same person twice in his lifetime. The problem, therefore, when teaching and learning skills, is to determine the acceptable parameters of accuracy for a given moment, keeping in mind the social, aesthetic, and practical demands on the performer.

3. Performance curves containing a plateau or even decreased improvement can often be made to evidence further improvement by spacing the practice trials.
4. The mentally retarded or less capable performer may experience little task inhibition when confronted with tasks which to most would appear simple. He thus may evidence marked improvement when practice trials are massed in time, while average individuals would not.
5. Whole practice is best because it usually results in more rapid learning. As much of a task as possible should be presented to capable performers.
6. When tasks are extremely complex and/or when the performer is less capable intellectually or physically, part practice or progressive-part practice may be called for.
7. If possible, practice at full speed should be attempted when the skill is not dangerous, complex, or disorienting to the learner. If the skill is reasonably complex or involves some danger and/or disorientation in space, initial slow practice may be called for.

DISCUSSION QUESTIONS AND EXERCISES

1. Discuss the variety of possible spaced versus massed practice conditions with regard to practice trials and practice sessions.
2. What practice conditions—massed, spaced, or some combination of both—are best suited for what kinds of skill learning?
3. What kinds of skills are best learned under whole-practice conditions? What kinds of skills are best acquired under part or progressive-part conditions?
4. Select a novel complex skill. Teach it to another student under progressive-part practice conditions. Obtain feedback from an observing student concerning the effectiveness of your efforts. Obtain the same kind of information from the performer himself.
5. How might you space practice of basketball skills in a physical education class that meets every day?
6. Discuss what might constitute a whole skill to a young retardate; to an intellectually more capable adolescent.
7. Under what conditions would you teach first for accuracy versus speed? Under what conditions would you emphasize speed initially? Under what conditions would you emphasize both speed and accuracy equally?
8. What factors would influence whether you initially emphasize speed or accuracy when teaching a motor skill?
9. Practice a novel skill under massed practice conditions. Contrast the performance curve to one obtained from another performer who is permitted a rest between trials.

10. Discuss the concept of work–rest ratio. What factors might influence the effect of this ratio on ultimate learning?

BIBLIOGRAPHY

AMMONS, R. B., "Acquisition of Motor Skill: III. Effects of Initially Distributed Practice on Rotary Pursuit Performance," *J. Exp. Psych.*, XL (1950), 777.

AMMONS, R. B., and WILLIG, LESLIE, "Acquisition of Motor Skills: IV. Effects of Repeated Periods of Massed Practice," *J. Exp. Psych.*, LI (1956), 2.

CRATTY, BRYANT J., "Practice Factors, Learning and Retention," in *Movement Behavior and Motor Learning* (2nd ed.). Philadelphia: Lea & Febiger, 1967.

———, "Practice," in *Psychology and Physical Activity*. Englewood Cliffs, N.J.: Prentice-Hall, Inc., 1968.

CRATTY, BRYANT J., and HUTTON, ROBERT S., "Whole Versus Part Practice" and "Spaced Versus Distributed Practice," Experiments 16 and 17 in *Experiments in Movement Behavior and Motor Learning*. Philadelphia: Lea & Febiger, 1969.

KNAPP, B., "Factors Affecting the Acquisition of Skill," Chapter 4 in *Skill in Sport*. London: Routledge and Kegan Paul, 1963.

LAWTHER, JOHN D., "Practice and Factors Affecting Its Influence on Motor Learning," in *The Learning of Physical Skills*. Englewood Cliffs, N.J.: Prentice-Hall, Inc., 1968.

SAGE, GEORGE H., "Conditions Affecting Motor Skill Acquisition and Performance: Practice," in *Introduction to Motor Behavior: A Neuropsychological Approach*. Reading, Mass.: Addison-Wesley Publishing Co., Inc., 1971.

SINGER, ROBERT N., "Teaching Methodology," in *Motor Learning and Human Performance*. New York: The Macmillan Company, 1968.

6

Motivation and Activation

It is a common observation that when people try harder, the manner in which they learn and perform motor skill seems to change in various ways. It is also obvious that people choose to perform, or not to perform, an endless variety of movement activities both at work and at play.

The terms *activation* and *arousal* are often employed to describe something about the intensity with which an individual performs a motor or mental task; *motivation* and *motives* are employed to denote the reasons why people choose to perform certain motor skills while avoiding others.

There are at least two main problems to be discussed in this chapter: whether and why an individual selects to engage in a task or tasks, and how hard he tries once he decides on a course of action. Two measures of the second problem are how much effort he applies and how long he endures in a given task situation.

Many terms and phrases are commonly employed to denote the same parameters of behavior. Coaches are constantly attempting to determine how they can get an athlete or an entire team "up" for a contest. Most discussions among coaches include at least one reference to how athletes can be motivated to perform well in sports.

MOTIVATION

Motivation Viewed Developmentally

Some authorities have suggested that infants are born with the need for movement in varying degrees. Active infants usually become active and vigorous adults, according to researchers who have measured the same people from birth to maturity.

As the child matures, he becomes increasingly specific in his movement preferences. As he reaches middle childhood he usually becomes interested in some activities and rejects others. By the age of eight, boy–girl preferences in sports and games become discernible; by adolescence, a variety of cultural pressures, sanctions, and rewards mold the youthful choices of both sexes.

Motivation can be measured in various ways using children and youth of various ages and of both sexes. For example, through the use of an attitude scale we can attempt to determine the degree to which the respondents like physical activity or physical education in general ways; we might prefer to survey the degree to which a group of boys, girls, or adults prefer to participate in specific activities. Another problem is to determine at which ages certain motives seem likely to influence motor performance either positively or negatively. For example, it seems that before age five, various kinds of social incentives, while exciting the child, do little to enhance his actual performance scores; after six and until age twelve, however, verbal encouragement and/or tangible rewards will positively influence performance in a variety of motor tasks including measures of fitness. By late childhood and early adolescence, youths seem more likely to be positively influenced in their efforts by qualities inherent in the task rather than by external rewards of various kinds. In other words, by adolescence interest in the task itself rather than other, more apparent rewards is more important.

Types of Rewards and Their Influence on Motor Performance

Rewards or motives for selecting and participating in motor activities take a number of forms, and their influence probably extends from birth. For example, a recent study carried out by a student of mine revealed a significant and reasonably high correlation between parent attitudes about physical activity and physical education and the physical performance scores of their children. Other conditions which reward infants a few days old and remain influential later in life are characteristics within the task itself which make it attractive and make children eager to engage in it. These qualities, explored in research on human and animal subjects, are discussed below.

The Complexity of the Task

Most children and youths seek to engage in optimally complex tasks which offer them some challenge. Presented with tasks which are too simple, for example, drawing a circle, children frequently embellish the tasks (drawing a face in the circle). Left to their own devices, children and youths complicate the rules of games which they perceive as too simple and not challenging enough. Children and adults, it has been hypothesized, have definite needs for mastering tasks, which can be met only if the tasks are reasonably difficult.

Novelty

Experiments on monkeys and children have produced data illustrating how a new or novel experience attracts performers and encourages more vigorous participation. Tasks may be completely different from past experience or they may be a novel form of an activity in which individuals have engaged in the past.

PSYCHOLOGICAL NEEDS AND MOTIVES

The Need to Struggle to Overcome Obstacles

Another sometimes powerful motive to engage in physical tasks, particularly in those which require all-out strength and/or endurance, may be the need to perform a task for the sheer feeling of engaging in a difficult struggle. It has been suggested, for example, that man is a stress-seeking animal. Obviously, people possess this need to overcome adversity to varying degrees, depending on their inherent physical constitution, their past experience in physically taxing situations, and the rewards they have received when they have taxed themselves to their physical limits.

Teachers and coaches of physical skills should recognize this basic need and attempt to help individuals satisfy it in physical tasks which are taxing but which do not overstress their constitutions.

The Need to Exhibit Excellence

Some writers hold that modern societies place great emphasis on the seeking and exhibition of excellence in some field. Everyone seems to need to be at least reasonably good at "his thing." It has been further explained that youthful abilities permit the young to excel in physical tasks, whereas their relatively short lifespan does not always permit them to excel in activities requiring academic background and high levels of experience and intelligence. This observation has been employed to explain why participation in sports activities is so attractive to the younger members of a society.

The Need for Status

Most lists of psychological needs include the need for status. In many high schools and colleges at least a minimum amount of status is connected with physical performance. Indeed, even in younger children we can see that at least a minimal amount of motor skill is needed for even limited social acceptance by a child's peers. Conversely, clumsy children often report that they are not important members of their class, that their friends make fun of them, and that boys or girls do not like them.

Affiliation Needs

Participation and membership in sports teams and in other types of social organizations to some degree meet the needs for affiliation of children and youths. Not only do people need status among their peers, they also need to be or to feel "a part of the group." The closeness or "we-feeling" of sports groups increases to the degree to which the team is successful, so that separating the needs for mastery, status, and affiliation according to their impact as separate motivating forces is often difficult.

TANGIBLE REWARDS

Professional athletes constantly try to negotiate better contracts so that they will make more money for their efforts. To some degree, the monetary rewards influence their decision to remain in the professional ranks and mold how hard they try when competing.

Children and youths compete in a variety of circumstances for obvious tangible rewards. Monetary or material rewards have been shown to have some influence over a child's choice to participate in a task and over how hard he works at that task. Several important considerations relate to "bribes" of this nature:

1. Do the rewards offered have value to those being rewarded, or are they only perceived as rewards by those who offer them?
2. At what point will a child become satiated with the reward? For example, while a child may perform more push-ups when offered a candy reward for excellence, at what point will further candy have little or no effect on his performance?
3. Is improvement as seen by the teacher compatible with improvement as seen by the students? In one study, for example, a group of students who were permitted to obtain their reward when *they* felt they had improved posted greater overall gains than a group which received rewards from an experimenter when *he* believed they had improved.

SOCIAL MOTIVES AND REWARDS

There are a number of obvious social rewards and punishments for good and bad performance in physical activities and athletics. Some athletes perform well when rewarded with the accolades of the fans, while others seek the approval of their friends and family. Most people perform motor skills, if not better, at least differently before an audience. Most of us go to great lengths when performing motor tasks to avoid disapproval or "razzing" from those who are important to us.

The youngster's social atmosphere generally sanctions participation in certain activities while offering less approval for others. The daughters of affluent parents, for example, may be offered tennis and swimming lessons, although their participation in football and basketball may not be as highly applauded by parents and friends. The ghetto youth often sees success in athletics as one of the only legitimate ways to get ahead, while the more economically favored youth sees his participation in high school athletics as only one of the ways to help him achieve a college or university education.

Some writers have suggested that even when a child performs in solitude, he is conscious of an unseen audience of friends, peers, and coaches, who might at a later date judge his performance as inadequate, adequate, or superior compared to others of his sex and age. Some are more influenced by social rewards than others. Scores on personality tests which indicate "needs for social approval" reflect this tendency to seek praise or not to be concerned about what others think of performance.

In any case, certain guidelines help us classify, and at times to discern, the possible effects of various kinds of social motives on physical performance:

1. "Razzing" by close and important friends has a marked disrupting effect on the performance of motor skills. However, the presence of disliked peers has been shown to have a positive effect on skill, as the performer seems to be trying to show the unfriendly observer how well he can perform.
2. Simple, direct acts performed before audiences are usually performed better, if they are not already being performed at capacity; however, complex skills which have not been well learned may suffer disruption in the same situation. Skills which have been overlearned are less likely to be disturbed as the individual performs in front of an audience.
3. Competition becomes an important motive under several conditions, including the desire on the part of two or more people to excel at the same activity, the feeling on the part of these individuals that each has a chance to win, and the perception on the part of each competitor that his opponent is not too much better or worse than he is.

    Arranging competitive circumstances, however, does not always guarantee more intensive or effective motor performance. Clumsy children, for example, are not usually motivated when they are continually placed in situations in which they stand a good chance to lose. Highly anxious individuals, as well as those with low levels of anxiety, may not be able to tolerate competitive circumstances. Individuals who know how well or how poorly they will do as compared to others present are less likely to be highly motivated when they are asked to compete.

    Physical education teachers and coaches are usually by nature competitive people, particularly in physical performance situations. It has been found that most competitive people (1) perceive others to be competitive, whether they are or not, and (2) perceive people who are not physically competitive as being somehow immoral or lacking in character. If the teacher of physical education cannot accommodate to individual differences in the inclination to compete, his teaching behavior may be less than effective.
4. Individuals differ markedly in the need to affiliate with others on an athletic team. Some join teams primarily to obtain and enjoy close affiliation with others; to other people team membership provides a vehicle through which they can satisfy motives to achieve, to master, and to perform well in a given sport. Some studies have found that if the affiliative need is too high, team performance may suffer. Of course, a

team which is under constant tension because of poor social relationships among members is not likely to do well. There seems to be an optimum amount of social tension between team members which is productive of the best effort.

5. While superior athletes seem to be aware of the social rewards and status which their fans confer on them by financial and personal support of their efforts, many do not like the fans. Obviously, fans are fickle, applauding one day and rejecting less successful efforts the next. Athletes' dislike of their fans also seems to stem from the athletes' feelings that the fans trade on their performance to obtain vicarious success, while sharing little of the athletes' anguish during the game and work during practice sessions.

6. Vocal social approval is likely to have a mixed effect on a group of athletes. For the effect to be positive, the one giving it must be respected by the performers. Vocal approval cannot be extended too often or it will lose its impact; at the same time, negative aspects of the situation may reduce or eliminate the positive effects of verbal exhortation.

MEASURING MOTIVES AND TEACHER SENSITIVITY

Effective teachers constantly search for what motivates the students in their physical education classes. The search can be carried on by constructing a questionnaire listing items which might to varying degrees "help you to learn and perform best in my class." These items may be suggested by the students; samples might include "opportunity to practice," "competitions," "written material on the sport," "chance to observe good performers."

After each item on the questionnaire the teacher or coach should place the numbers one through nine, so that the student can circle the number indicating the degree to which a given item helps him do well. A single item might appear like this:

	of little help								of great help
Opportunity to play games	1	2	3	4	5	6	7	8	9

After the questionnaire has been administered to the class, a profile can be computed averaging the students' scores on each item. Before averaging, the teacher should attempt to judge for himself the "weight" to be assigned to each item, in other words, to determine how sensitive he is to the degree to which various situations motivate his students. Thus, he can contrast what he thinks is motivating his students most, with what the students actually indicate. When I tried this evaluation exercise,

I was surprised that, for example, competition was not as highly judged by my college-age students as it was by me. They already knew how well they would do in a competitive situation, and gave higher marks to such items as "an opportunity to improve yourself." Perhaps you, too, will find similar discrepancies between what you think is motivating your future students or team performers and what they report on such a questionnaire.

Motives to perform physical tasks well are numerous and complex. Motives to perform well, and problems which may block performance, come from within the individual (his psychological needs), from outside sources (tangible rewards or social approval of various types), and from the task itself (novelty, complexity).

Any motive or combination of motives may "turn on" a performer; the positive strength of one motive may counteract the negative effects of another. For example, last on a high school girl's hierarchy of worthwhile physical activities (motive emanating from the task) is marching. Yet put a pompon in her hand and place her on a football field at halftime with the rest of a drill team (social motives), and she may march until exhaustion.

The effects of specific motives are transitory. Not only do they differ during an individual's lifetime, but various motives may exert different effects on performance during a single day or week. Thus, to assess the motives which may stimulate performance in a given physical endeavor, one must obtain a great deal of formal and informal information about the individual whose value system one wishes to understand.

ACTIVATION

Activation is reflected in the intensity with which an individual pursues a task. Measures of activation include various physiological indices such as changes in muscular tension, heart-rate, respiration, and the like, which indicate that the individual is preparing himself to act or to meet some perceived threat, and measures which indicate that the body is ceasing functions which might be unnecessary for meeting a threat or becoming active. The digestive movements of the stomach usually slow down or cease when an individual is activated, for example.

Average or moderate levels of activation usually result in the best effort in complex motor skills. Early studies including three groups—one which was asked to exert extra tension, a second which was asked to relax, and a third which was left alone—usually showed that becoming too relaxed or too tense inhibited performance.

Further, it is usually found that there is an optimum level of activation or arousal which results in the best performance for a given task; if the individual is either over- or underactivated, less than optimum performance is realized. This rule holds for most forms of athletic competition, and is often related to specific positions on a team. For example, the levels of activation needed by interior linemen in football, who move directly and forcefully, are often higher than those required by the quarterback, whose tasks require careful and exact coordination and complex judgments.

There is an important social dimension to the study of interrelationships between activation level and physical performance. Activation is "catching" among team members, class members, and between the teacher-coach and those he directs. Excitable coaches may overexcite certain team members; players who are too activated may likewise raise the activation levels of other team members in close physical proximity. Highly individual physical and behavioral differences are exhibited as people become activated. Some people may, for example, exhibit muscular tension changes, while others may not. Some may show signs of physiological unrest (high heartbeat), while others do not to the same degree. Some individuals may experience muscular tension changes within specific muscular groups, for example, around the head and neck, while others may exhibit muscular tension changes only in the larger muscles of the limbs and back. Some when overly activated prefer to pace up and down, while others may become almost rigid and experience varying degrees of immobility.

Therefore, if one hopes to adjust an individual's or a team's level of activation to optimum levels before the performance of a motor task or before a game, several considerations should be kept in mind:

1. What is the individual's habitual level of activation?
2. What signs indicate that the performer may be either over- or underactivated, relative to task demands?
3. What are the demands of the task, relative to the optimum level of activation needed? Where is the performer relative to these demands?
4. What influence has past exposure to activating conditions (an audience, for example) had on the performance about to occur?
5. What kinds of techniques might be most effective in adjusting the individual's level of activation?

Techniques which have been applied either to activate or to deactivate an athletic performer range from those which have been well researched to those which are more folklore than fact. Some of the methods can be applied by the untrained or by the athlete himself, while others require an individual well versed in their use, even someone possessing an advanced degree in clinical psychology or in pharmacology. The effectiveness of any of these methods depends on the skill and insight of the individual applying them, relative to the situation and the athlete. Some athletes require more than one approach, while others need only a single "remedy." Techniques which seem to work during the initial part of a sports season may not be as effective later in the season. Some of the methods require direct physical reactions on the part of the athlete, for example, relaxation training; others depend more on altering the mind-set of the individual by offering him information which may activate or deactivate him in various ways. Some of the methods are discussed below.

Adjusting the Importance of the Contest

Athletes are often over- or underactivated because they place distorted importance on the impending contest. The efforts of highly excited high school and college athletes may be made more reasonable by pointing out to them how many other high schools in the country happen to be playing football on a given Friday, or, as one coach mentioned to the starting quarterback just before the Rose Bowl game, "Eight hundred million Chinese really don't care at all what will happen here today!" Of course, the reverse psychology will be needed when athletes appear underactivated before a contest; they should be told that a great deal depends on their good efforts in the game.

Adjusting the Social Conditions

Athletes who are too highly activated may need to be isolated from others who may be adversely affected by their excitement. The coach should attempt to keep his emotional state from the athlete, whom he might further upset before a contest. Underactivated athletes may need to be placed in close proximity to those who are activated to ideal levels.

"Obliterating" the Contest

A professional ice hockey star with whom I recently conversed said that at times the team played a game of bridge before games, when tensions seemed high. The coach attempted to keep their minds off the impending contest by giving them a rigorous intellectual test, one which would not permit much thought about anything other than the task at hand.

Relaxation Training (Psychotonic Training)

Using techniques first advanced to reduce the tensions of emotionally upset individuals, many athletes and sports psychologists around the world engage in training which helps to reduce residual muscular tensions that often accompany unusually high states of activation. They are taught to relax, to tighten their muscles, and then to "let go," and to attempt to isolate parts of their bodies where extra residual muscle tensions may be accumulating.

Although the claims made about relaxation training are in advance of available research, it has been suggested that this technique may be used not only to calm the athlete who is too excited, but also to help the underaroused athlete attain higher, optimum levels of activation. To raise activation level, the athlete is first calmed down, through relaxation techniques, and then urged (usually vocally) to higher levels of activation. The process is then repeated several times to lower tension and then to arouse. It is claimed that in this manner athletes may be more aroused than when attempts are made to "get him up" by starting at his base level of arousal-activation.

Help the Performer Understand and Accept Signs of Activation

A supposedly antiquated theory of emotion suggests that we assume an emotional state because we see ourselves exhibiting some kind of behavior. For example, we believe ourselves sad when we see ourselves cry. The same phenomenon may occur before athletic competition, which may be accompanied by signs of nervousness like palm sweating, to which the athlete might overreact—"look at my hands—I must be frightened!" Coaches who are confronted with this type of problem report that to handle it, they help the athlete understand that the signs often indicate that helpful levels of activation are being reached, rather than that some kind of personality disintegration is occurring.

SUMMARY

Activation refers to the intensity with which individuals perform motor tasks. It could be evaluated by measuring foot-pounds of work or the duration of time an individual is willing to perform. The study of motivation deals with the reasons for which people choose to perform certain tasks.

Motivation with regard to physical activity is probably highly generalized during infancy and early childhood and revolves around inherent needs to be active to varying degrees. In later childhood and adolescence, specific types of activities are selected; the reasons for engaging in them emanate increasingly from the tasks themselves, from the novelty and complexity perceived as inherent in various kinds of physical performances.

Several types of motives apparently impel us to perform physical tasks: various types of social motives, such as the need for status, for affiliation, and for recognition; motives which are more personal or psychological in nature, such as the desire to master a task or to stress oneself physically; and material payments and rewards, which exert a mixed influence on performance, and, if overused, tend to have reduced effects on people's selection of tasks and their effort in those tasks.

Both overactivation and underactivation relative to a task's requirements are likely to reduce performance efficiency. Adjusting arousal-activation downward is sometimes more difficult than increasing activation, although in prolonged sports seasons, the latter is often a distinct problem.

The adjustment of activation levels can be accomplished by adjusting social conditions (isolating a too-excited performer from the rest of the team), by administering medication, or by attempting to change the performer's perceptions of the situation by playing up or playing down the importance of the impending competition.

DISCUSSION QUESTIONS AND EXERCISES

1. Contrast the concepts of motivation and activation. In a sports situation, what behaviors would give evidence of each?
2. What motives might be important to twelve-year-old boys performing physical fitness tests?
3. In what ways might a program of physical education be made more motivating to girls in early adolescence? Why might it be difficult to motivate girls of this age to perform vigorously?
4. What might a coach do before a contest to help a boy lower his level of activation? What might he do to help a boy heighten his level of activation?
5. What factors influence levels of activation, and also influence a coach's decision to try to heighten or lessen an individual's level of activation?
6. What physical signs may show that boys or girls are too aroused to perform well?

7. List motives which are social in nature, those which are psychological in character, and those which are more physiologically oriented.
8. How may extrinsic rewards (prizes or money) be effective and ineffective as motivators? Under what conditions are intrinsic motives (interest in the task) most effective modifiers of motor behavior?
9. Apply relaxation training techniques to a classmate. In what ways might this training need to be modified for the younger child, the Olympic athlete, the retarded youngster?
10. How may performer's thoughts heighten or lessen levels of activation?

BIBLIOGRAPHY

APPLEY, MORTIMER H., and TRUMBULL, RICHARD, *Psychological Stress.* New York: Appleton-Century-Crofts, 1967.

BEISSER, ARNOLD R., *The Madness in Sports.* New York: Appleton-Century-Crofts, 1967.

CRATTY, BRYANT J., "Social Motives," Chapter 9 in *Movement Behavior and Motor Learning* (2nd ed.). Philadelphia: Lea & Febiger, 1967.

———, "Attention, Activation, and Self-Control," Chapter 7 in *Human Behavior: Exploring Educational Processes.* Wolfe City, Tex.: University Press, 1971.

DUFFY, ELIZABETH, *Activation and Behavior.* New York: John Wiley & Sons, Inc., 1962.

JACOBSON, EDMUND, *Progressive Relaxation.* Chicago: The University of Chicago Press, 1938.

MASLOW, ABRAHAM H., *Motivation and Personality.* New York: Harper & Row, Publishers, 1954.

7

Intelligence and Skill Acquisition

References to the integration of mind and body are frequent in the philosophical literature of the Greeks and Romans. Indeed, produced during those centuries were statues, still extant, which combine intelligent countenances with well-proportioned, muscular bodies.

The search for the relationship between intellectual and movement behaviors is also seen in the efforts of the first experimental psychologists in Germany, the United States, and England. While their first efforts were often directed toward the discovery of various perceptual differences in their subjects, later attempts were often directed toward trying to measure intelligence through the administration of basic sensory and motor tests of various kinds. And although these early efforts to predict intellectual performance by assessing motor traits failed, several studies since that time have attempted to link the intellectual and movement components of the human personality.

Relationships between intelligence and motor skill learning can be studied in several ways. For example, we can attempt to determine whether simply thinking about a task will improve skill acquisition. Some have tried to discover links between the possession and improvement of motor abilities in children and their ability to carry out intellectual endeavors.

Fitness and measures of academic performance and skill learning have interested researchers throughout the years; descriptions of the use of movement activities to modify the social, emotional, and intellectual behaviors of retarded and neurologically impaired children are frequent.

Sports psychologists, particularly those in Eastern Europe, have attempted to determine what kinds of intellectual training may support, sustain, and heighten athletic success in various sports. Scholars in this country and abroad have begun to devise vigorous games to enhance such academic competences as reading, spelling, and mathematics. Still others have begun to look deeper, attempting to determine how various basic intellectual processes including problem-solving, memorization, evaluation, and categorization can be translated into motivating movement activities.[1]

I have attempted in this chapter to provide material which illustrates how intellectual behavior may interact specifically with motor skills, and to describe the practical ways in which the teacher might employ both his own intelligence and that of his charges when attempting to elicit higher level motor performance. Specifically, this chapter deals with mental practice and its interaction with physical practice in skill acquisition, with the theoretical and practical ways in which motor skill learning and physical fitness interact with academic attainment, with the ways in which various types of intellectual preparation may be incorporated into the training regimes of athletes, and with the practical implications of these topics for teachers and coaches of physical education.

Intellectual Components of Motor Skill Learning

To deny the existence of thought within the motor skill learning process is unrealistic and nonproductive. In varying degrees of sophistication, performers of motor skills think about what they are attempting, why they are doing it, and what will be the consequences of their behavior. Several dimensions of this intellectual behavior are worthy of consideration: (1) What does the performer think about; that is, does an individual have a visual image of his performance, or does he translate thought and movement into words? (2) What are his thoughts before the task, during its execution and between trials, and following his performance, in the way of personal evaluation of success or failure? (3) What is the quality of the thought underlying task performance, that is, how specific it is to the task, what mechanical analysis takes place, and so on?

Research on mental practice during the past thirty years has been highly supportive of the worth of thinking about tasks before their execu-

---

[1] For a more penetrating look at this general problem area, see Bryant J. Cratty, *Physical Expressions of Intelligence* (Englewood Cliffs, N.J.: Prentice-Hall, Inc., 1972).

tion and between performance trials. Groups of subjects who are instructed in detail, but not at too much length, what to think about the performance of a given skill (for example, "imagine yourself swinging the bat levelly") perform better than those who receive no such instruction. However, such findings result from experiments in which subjects are instructed how to think while performing; they are not based on the spontaneous thoughts of the performers themselves.

It is never found that mental practice is superior to physical practice. Instead, there is usually an optimum combination of physical and mental practice, usually a two to one ratio of physical to mental practice. Mental practice is most productive during the initial stages of skill learning rather than during intermediate or final stages. Indeed, one study indicates that the benefits of mental practice equal those of physical practice during the early stages of skill acquisition.

The more sophisticated studies usually involve a combination of physical practice conditions: for example, permitting one group simply to observe a task being performed, telling a second group to practice the skill mentally, and giving a third group actual physical practice. A fourth (control) group is usually denied chances to observe or to perform the task physically or mentally. The findings in these studies usually appear as in Figure 7.1.

The group having no opportunity to practice or to observe usually performs poorest on a test–retest. The "observation group" shows a little more improvement, but the most improvement is seen in the groups that have physical or mental practice, with the former usually outperforming the latter.

Within normal ranges, scores on intelligence tests do not seem predictive of the effect of mental practice on motor skill performance. It is difficult to determine which types of skills seem to be influenced most by mental practice.

Both central and peripheral theories are offered to explain why mental practice may aid skill learning. The peripheralists claim that minute muscular activity in the form of the skill itself accompanies mental practice. However, data to support the theory that the muscles "fire" in the same order and relative intensity during mental practice of the skill, as they would if the skill were practiced physically, are difficult to come by.

It is likely that mental practice indeed activates important processes within the central nervous system to initiate an accurate "motor program," and that the formation and activation of a program transfers to the physical manifestation of the skill when it is eventually begun.

In any case, the implications of this research for the coach and physical education instructor are obvious:

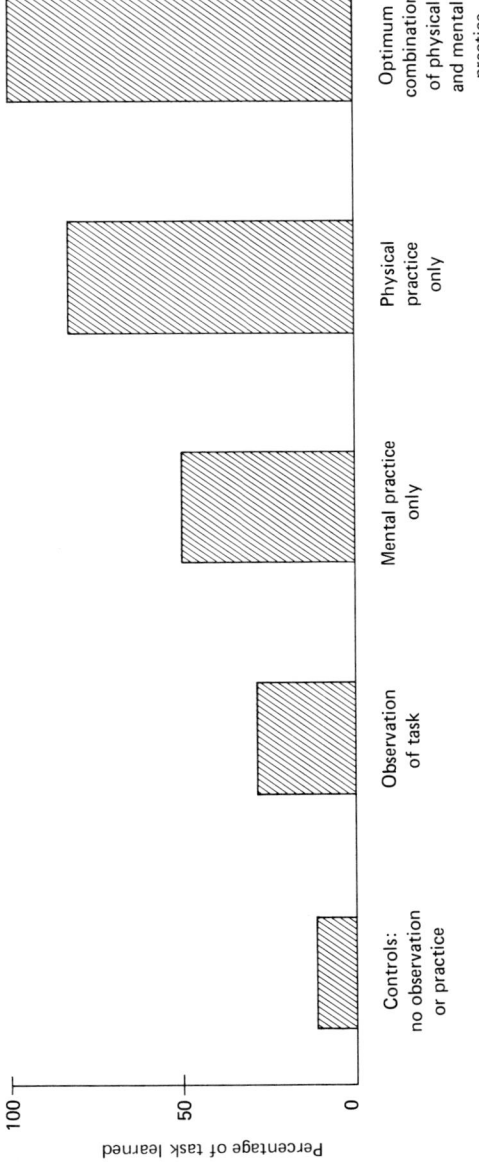

Figure 7.1

1. Skill learning will be enhanced to the extent to which the participating children think about the task and watch others perform while they themselves are not actively engaged.
2. A combination of physical and mental practice is usually best, depending on the intellectual complexity of the skill, the maturity of the learners, their attention span, and similar variables.
3. Mental practice effects are highest during the initial periods of skill learning, when the individual must analyze the task and cognitively integrate the various submovements.
4. When individuals instruct themselves in a skill, they are usually concentrating only on a single task component at any given time.

Fitness, Academic Performance, and Intelligence

Although there has been much speculation recently that participation by young children in motor skill activities will enhance their intellectual potentials, research has not strongly supported such speculation. However, there *are* interesting ways in which motor skill development, fitness, and intellectual potential may interact.

For example, studies carried out in Scandinavia found that fitness and reading ability were not highly correlated in the lower elementary grades, but that in the higher elementary grades, the more intelligent children did tend also to be more fit. The investigators suggested that during the early school years the more passive, scholarly types seemed to be more likely to spend time reading, while the more active tended to play more games; later, as the games became more complex and challenging, they began to attract the attention of able children, raising their fitness levels.

The same research program also found that if fit children were confined to classroom situations which restricted their opportunities for movement all day, they began to bring less intellectual effort to the tasks placed before them than did children with lower fitness scores, who may have possessed lower needs for physical activity. These findings, based on IQ tests given successively throughout the school day, indicate that children with high activity needs and fitness levels may need more activity breaks than others, to ensure their best academic performance.

Studies with adults in various parts of the world have also related fitness, exercise, and academic performance. Mild to moderate exercise will put the highly fit individual in a relaxed state, in which he is likely to do better on various academic tests. On the other hand, a less fit individual who is made to do vigorous exercise will often find the activity not only taxing but stressful and will probably perform less well on academic activities than he would have prior to his exposure to exercise.

Studies in Sweden indicate that better performance in mathematic computation is elicited from subjects who have been exercised to a moderate degree on a treadmill (45 percent maximum) while listening to math problems through earphones, than from subjects either standing still or exercised at 80 percent maximum. Also, when hyperactive children have an opportunity to rest and relax following vigorous activity, their academic work is better than if they are overaroused in games and then led directly into the classroom.

The findings have the following implications for teachers of physical education and coaches:

1. To challenge more intelligent youngsters and to elicit their best effort in physical activities, one must present them with games which contain an intellectual challenge. The rules must be reasonably complex or the teacher must provide opportunities for the children to experiment with different rules, new apparatus, or even the invention of new games.
2. The amount of exercise given to children and youths must be compatible with their fitness levels. Physical fitness programs of gradually increasing intensity should be offered so that children are not suddenly subject to exercise stress to which their systems cannot accommodate. Programs that stress them limit their intellectual potential in the hours which follow activity.
3. Hyperactive children, who cannot seem to calm down after physical education periods to levels compatible with good classroom work, may need special relaxation training at the end of the physical education period; such training will permit them to lower their activation and muscular tension to levels compatible with good functioning in the more passive classroom environment.

INTELLECTUAL DEMANDS IN ATHLETICS

It is usually found that there is no precise correlation between intelligence measures and athletic success in the more complex sports, although at least a minimal amount of intelligence is needed to perform well, to understand the rationale underlying training regimes, and to deal with team and individual strategies while competing. However, at least two intellectual dimensions of sport should be considered, to produce good to superior performances: (1) Various sports make specific intellectual demands, which, if trained for, will often produce more obvious success. (2) General information on sports psychology, physiology of exercise, and the social psychology and sociology of sport participation may help athletes to know themselves better, to train, and to deal with the complexities of the sports environment.

Unfortunately, little evidence is available concerning the influence of either specific "ideomotor" training in a sports requirement or broadly-based general information about human performance. However, particularly in eastern Europe, some research has been done on this subject.

Tactical Training

Various formal and informal attempts may be made to instill in athletes the tactical "sense" they need for dealing with the complexities of a specific game. For example, in "chalk talks" the players are relatively passive, and are asked to think about their movements and the actions of their opponents in the game situation. "Slowed down" practices may be held so that players will learn to think about the movements of their opponents and teammates, and their reaction to each in the game situation. This approach is often employed with ice hockey and water polo teams, the members arranging themselves on a field or basketball court and walking or running through the movements, without having to concentrate on the demanding skating or swimming required in the two sports.

Tactical training may be carried out in preparation for individual sports as well as team sports. For example, coaches of swimmers or runners sometimes rehearse carefully how athletes will run against specific opponents, how teammates may try to "box" an opponent during a distance running race, or how and when to make a move in a swimming contest. Indeed, if tactical training is not practiced before such individual sports contests, less satisfactory meet performance is likely to ensue. Specific examples of individual-sport tactical training which may be incorporated into practice sessions include the following:

1. "Catch-up drills" in which a swimmer or runner is placed in a practice race a short distance behind another athlete and asked to catch up with and pass his opponent in a situation similar to that expected to occur in the competitive contest.
2. Quick passing drills, in which the athlete learns how to "explode" past an opponent in a swimming or running race. Practice may be aimed toward "quick" passing at specific points in a race, at given distances, or at given locations (on a turn, off a wall as in swimming, or on a straightaway). Generally quick passing drills should be carried out when the athlete is experiencing varying degrees of fatigue similar to those he will experience in the race for which he is training.
3. "Stay-ahead drills," similar to the catch-up drills, in which the athlete attempts to stay ahead of a runner or swimmer who may be varying his pace and attempting to overtake his opponent. Most drills of this nature involve forcing runners or swimmers to vary their effort by "breaking out" of the rhythmical pace learned in practices, particularly those in which interval training has played an important part.

Tactical Training **101**

Formal attempts have been made in Eastern Europe, during the past several years, to instill tactics in various team sports performers and to evaluate their tactical ability. Among the more impressive techniques is that of flashing sets of pictures of team situations (ice hockey, basketball, and soccer), briefly before an athlete, who must quickly respond to several questions:

1. What has happened just before the picture was taken; that is, where have the players come from? What have they just done? Where has the ball (puck) come from?
2. What happened just after the picture was taken? Where are the players going? What will they do? Where is the ball (puck) going?
3. What would I do in the tactical situation shown, if I were on defense? On offense?

Similar studies have been tried in the United States. With further

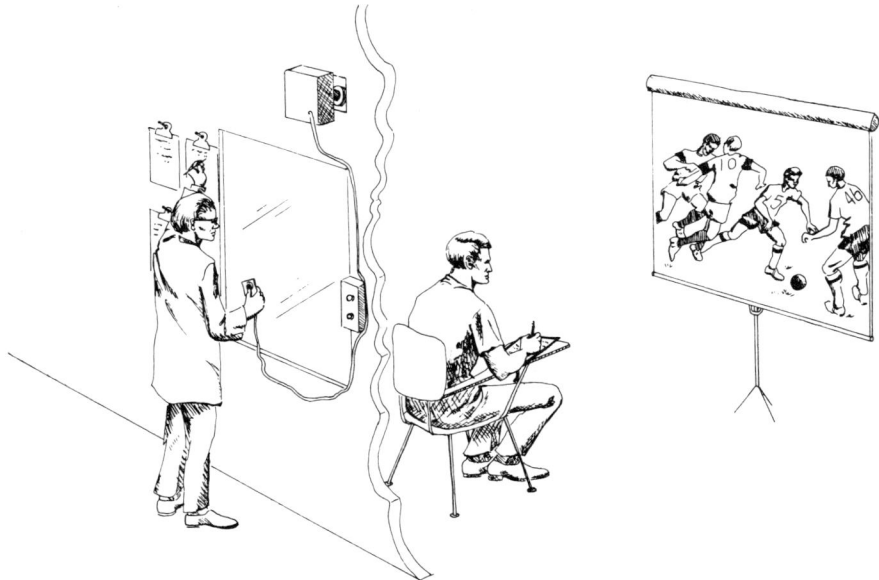

Figure 7.2 *Athletes' tactical abilities are often evaluated in experiments in which pictures of sports interactions are quickly flashed as shown. After the picture is no longer present, the athlete must determine what players were present, where the ball was, what the athletes were doing, what they probably will do next, what they probably did just prior to the picture, and what he would do in the situation. Reprinted by permission from* Psychology and the Superior Athlete, *by Bryant J. Cratty and Miroslav Vanek. Copyright © 1970, The Macmillan Company.*

data, this means of evaluating and attempting to improve tactical abilities among team-sport athletes may be more reliably assessed.

Memory

Some sports require to varying degrees that an athlete remember a series of movements or environmental signposts. Slalom skiing, for example, requires that a participant quickly memorize the order of the gates through which he must pass; often the time he has to memorize is brief—as he ascends the hill for his first turn on an unfamiliar course.

Divers and some jumpers or vaulters in track and field mentally rehearse the movements they will make, attempting to "program in" the required actions with greater exactitude than if they did no preperformance rehearsal.

Data from mental practice studies employing triple jumpers and slalom skiers indicate that thinking about the specific movements one will make (triple jump), and generalized training in serial-memory ability (remembering a series of stimuli in correct order as in slalom skiing) have positive effects on sports performance. However, as many of these studies have been carried out in countries in which the statistical treatment and interpretation of psychological data are still in their infancy, more exact guidelines await sophisticated investigations still to come.

Closely associated with such studies are those in which attempts are made to instill "time sense" into athletes. In several athletic events, particularly middle- and long-distance swimming and diving, an awareness of pace is a vital part of the total performance effort. In general, the studies indicate that with practice, athletes acquire a remarkable ability to judge how fast they are racing, and at the completion of a race, to state how much time they have required to cover a given distance. Superior athletes are more proficient at this awareness of pace, and have better time sense, than the inexperienced.

Preparation of the athlete should not be begun the day or even the week of the contest. Mental components of athletic skill practice should become a regular part of his training regime and should be included with the physical components of the practices on a daily basis throughout the training season. Indeed, bringing the athlete's attention to these rather subtle but important mental details of performance suddenly, just before a contest, is probably more disruptive than helpful.

Mental rehearsal of complex physical skills before their execution is helpful to performance. Pacing and time sense may be exactly learned, and are helpful in competitive efforts. Sports involving short-term or long-term memory should be trained for by practice in "stretching" the athlete's ability to remember increasing amounts of information.

General Information

In some countries of the world almost all athletes competing on national teams are graduates of high schools and universities. Thus, they come to competition with at least a basic understanding of the mechanisms of the human body, psychology, and simple mechanics. Such athletes are likely to be easier to coach as they can understand the physical and physiological underpinnings of their events and know themselves better within the competitive context.

However, younger athletes in the more developed countries, as well as athletes from some of the emerging nations, may lack a basic background in some of the psychological, sociological, physiological, and mechanical principles important within the athletic situation.

Particularly in eastern Europe, special sports clinics help the athlete learn more about himself so that his competitive efforts will be enhanced. Outstanding physiologists, psychologists, and kinesiologists accompany the national teams of many countries, telling the athletes how to enhance performance with reference to the specialists' particular fields.[2] The psychologist contributes his knowledge of human behavior, interpreting personality test data. The physiologist, either formally at group lectures or informally in personal conferences, tries to help athletes understand the rationale behind strength and endurance training programs, as well as the principles governing an adequate diet. In some countries sociologists and social psychologists also work with teams in group situations and by means of lectures, to help athletes work more harmoniously in groups.[3]

Although no "hard" data confirm the effectiveness of the measures outlined above in improving sports performance, it would seem that the result of such special attention to the general academics behind athletic participation would be beneficial, although scientists at large sports centers in eastern Europe often seem to dwell on minutiae, and some American coaches are even amused, on visiting such countries, to be continually asked the "wrong" questions by their hosts! Even so, attention to the general intellectual underpinnings of sports performance should prove helpful.

[2] It was recently reported to me that the U.S.S.R. has a special psychologist solely for its competitive divers.

[3] I recently spoke to a group of over two hundred Canadian National Coaches, assembled for five days to hear lectures and take part in discussions on the physiological and psychological principles governing practical problems in coaching.

Several basic questions relate to putting scientific information about athletic performance into the proper context:

1. How much of a coach's scientific knowledge, obtained on his own or from scientific advisors, should be transmitted to the athlete? The athlete should not be confused by innumerable scientific findings, some of which are contradictory. Findings should be carefully screened, evaluated, and then presented to the athlete in terms he can understand and in ways which are helpful to him.
2. How should scientific team advisors work as a group to give proper emphasis to psychological versus physiological information? What part should the coach play in this interpretative and screening phase?
3. Where will the coach obtain the most valid, useful information to help him understand himself and his athletes?
4. What percentage of a coach's time and effort should be devoted to learning the "whys" and "hows" of athletic endeavor, and how much to actual application of what is known?

The questions are not easy to answer; however, by carefully considering them, the coach should become better able to obtain superior performance from his athletes, and the physical educator should likewise become able to elicit superior performance from his students.

DISCUSSION QUESTIONS AND EXERCISES

1. How would you optimize mental practice effects on skill learning?
2. Write how you would encourage a performer to practice a task mentally. What would you say to him?
3. How might a performer mentally practice a task?
4. What factors influence the effect of intellectual ability on motor skill learning?
5. How might mental processes retard motor skill learning?
6. What theories attempt to explain mental practice effects?
7. How might tactical training in complex game situations be conducted for team-sport athletes?
8. Design a day's schedule for an average elementary school, interpolating recess periods and in other ways accommodating to children with both high and low needs for activity.
9. Using various physical activity, how would you obtain the highest scores from highly fit youngsters on a test of intellectual ability?
10. How might you improve the academic abilities of youngsters with high needs for activity and little capacity to sit still in quiet classroom settings?

BIBLIOGRAPHY

CRATTY, BRYANT J., *Active Learning*. Englewood Cliffs, N.J.: Prentice-Hall, Inc., 1971.

———, "Cognitive Operations," Chapter 13 in *Human Behavior: Exploring Educational Processes*. Wolfe City, Tex.: University Press, 1971.

———, *Physical Expressions of Intelligence*. Englewood Cliffs, N.J.: Prentice-Hall, Inc., 1972.

GUILFORD, J. P., *Intelligence, Creativity, and their Educational Implications*. San Diego, Calif.: Robert R. Knapp, Publisher, 1968.

LEFFORD, ARTHUR, "Cognitive Factors in Skill Development," in K. J. Connolly, ed., *Mechanisms of Motor Skill Development*. New York: Academic Press, Inc., 1970.

VANEK, MIROSLAV, and CRATTY, BRYANT J., *Psychology and the Superior Athlete*. New York: The Macmillan Company, 1970.

WISEMAN, STEPHEN, ed., *Intelligence and Ability*. Baltimore: Penguin Books Inc., 1967.

8

Transfer of Skill

One of the most important categories of information involved in human skill acquisition is transfer of learning. The term *transfer* implies that the learning or performance of one or more tasks may have some influence, either negative or positive, on the learning or acquisition of one or more other tasks. Indeed, the extent to which school tasks are transferable or not transferable to other academic operations and to life experiences has for years been the topic of philosophical discussions about the nature of the total school curriculum.

Most teaching, whether in a classroom or a gymnasium, is based on the principle that transfer will take place. One learns algebra in the hope that the logic and coding inherent in its operations will transfer to adult intellectual operations. Within the physical realm, one practices basketball drills so that transfer will occur, and so that the total game will be played with efficiency.

The study of motor skill transfer can be divided in several ways. One may, for example, discuss the bilateral transfer of skill, by which a one-handed or one-footed task somehow influences the same or similar skills performed by another limb. "Within-individual" transfer has been the subject of several interesting studies over the past eighty years. A second classification of transfer effects is more important: the effect of practicing one task on the performance or learning of a second. In this case we are dealing with transfer between tasks instead of between the limbs of one individual.

There are many other classifications of transfer, for example, the extent to which verbal preparation before or during the motor task affects the level of skill acquired; the extent to which part-skill practice transfers to the whole skill; and the extent to which practicing a difficult skill seems to aid performance of its simpler components, or conversely, the extent to which practicing simple subskills enhances performance of the more complex whole.

An important subtopic is the optimization of positive transfer from one task to another, and conversely, the negative effects two tasks may have on each other when practiced in succession. Instructors usually try to practice tasks which will have the most desirable effects on a given sports skill, while reducing the possible negative effects of the acquisition of other skills.

A more subtle problem involves the difference between generalized transfer from one skill to another, and the transfer of specific elements of one task to another.

Another important subissue concerns the influence of stimulus and response elements within two tasks on possible transfer between them. Stimulus elements are primarily the visual conditions surrounding the task's performance (the ball approaching the catcher, movements of others in the field, and so on). Response elements are, of course, the movement and submovements which make up the task itself. Or, in other words, stimulus elements are input through the individual's senses, while response elements are the motor output, what he does in response to internalized commands and to the organization and interpretation of the input elements.

Answers to the important questions surrounding the transfer of skill often rest on analyses of several conditions interacting in the performance situation. This chapter attempts to clarify some of the principles governing the transfer of skill.

The Evaluation of Transfer Effects

The degree to which a drill or practice exercise transfers positively to a game situation can be judged by the coach or physical education instructor only subjectively. He may believe that a practice drill transfers positively to the game, but there can be no precise measurement, and numerous other variables may also improve game performance.

Within the laboratory, transfer has been explored thoroughly; however, while the purity of laboratory measurement conditions is high, laboratory tests often bear only slight resemblance to familiar sports skills. Several methods are employed within the laboratory to explore various kinds of transfer effects. For example, to identify possible generalized effects of

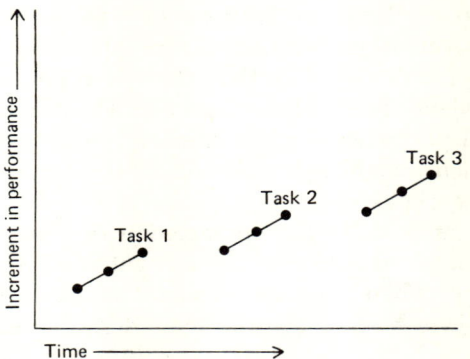

Figure 8.1

learning to learn (forming learning sets), a succession of tasks is given to subjects and it is noted if performance in each new task within the series begins at successively higher levels (see Figure 8.1).

More frequently, a group is given a series of trials in one task and then exposed to a second task to determine whether performers begin higher and remain better skilled than a second control group with no previous exposure to the second task. Figure 8.2 illustrates several types of data that may emerge from such studies.

Inspection of Figure 8.2 should not lead to the inference that prior practice of a task will necessarily produce positive transfer effects to a second task.

In summary, the effects of one task on another may be seen immediately or may be delayed, appearing in a measure of retention obtained after a prolonged period during which neither task has been practiced. Furthermore, transfer effects may be seen either in performance scores or when later learning curves are contrasted. If the initial practice task contains elements which are important during the early stages of acquisition of the second task, the transfer effects in the second task may be immediately apparent; on the other hand, if the elements in the first task practiced aid in the intermediate or final stages of skill learning in the second task, the transfer effects to the second may not be immediately apparent, but may emerge in the final trials of a series of practice efforts.

BILATERAL TRANSFER

Some of the earliest psychological experiments explored the apparent fact that "one hand teaches the other." In the 1930s studies even investigated the extent to which learning a motor task, or learning to move through various complex maze tasks, was transferable not only from hand to hand but from foot to hand, and vice versa.

A blindfolded subject, using a special shoe to which a writing instrument was attached, learned to move through a maze pattern consisting of a groove which transcribed an irregularly shaped pathway. The subject then attempted to move through the same pathway, again without vision, with the writing implement in his hand—sometimes in the hand on the same side as the foot that had been used, and sometimes in the opposite hand.

Such studies indicated, in general, that the most transfer occurred between hands, in one-handed tasks; intermediate amounts of transfer occurred from same-side hand to foot; and the least transfer from hands to feet or feet to hands on opposite sides of the body.

Later studies have produced conflicting results. For example, it is uncertain whether more transfer occurs from the preferred to the nonpreferred hand, or vice versa. Theories about transfer training between various limbs of the body are not fully illuminated by the current data. Some argue, for example, that while the subject practices with one hand, minute muscular tension changes which may be recorded in the opposite hand result in the installation of skill in the second hand. Others hold that certain mental or ideational elements in one-handed tasks cause transfer; that is, thinking about one-handed practice tends to cause transfer over the mental bridges formed between the tasks performed by either hand.

An interesting recent study confirms the second theoretical assumption. One group of subjects practiced a one-handed task and then attempted to perform the task with the opposite hand, evidencing the expected positive transfer; a second group of subjects, however, were permitted only to observe practice in the one-handed task before attempting it with one of their hands. That the skill level evidenced by the second group was similar to that of the first group, which had had prior physical practice, makes a strong case that the mental components of the task indeed caused the transfer effects seen in both groups.

The following guidelines seem valid for bilateral transfer:

1. Many complex one-handed skills contain numerous important intellectual elements to which learners and instructors should attend for efficient acquisition of those skills.
2. Observation as well as practice of one-handed skills may be productive.
3. Physical fatigue effects within a one-handed task may be circumvented and reasonably productive practice continued, in some cases, if practice is carried on by the second hand.

Transfer, either negative or positive, may be evaluated by inspecting performance scores and/or learning curves.

A. Performance Changes:
Group 1 (x) practices Task 1.

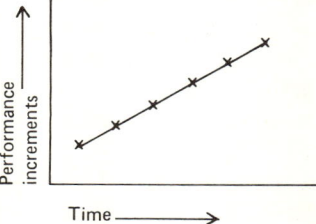

Performance on Task 2 by Group 1 (x), contrasted to performance of Group 2 (●).

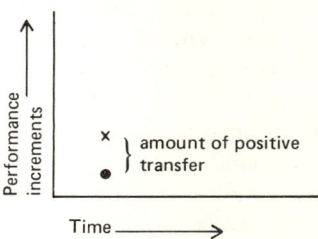

B. Learning Changes
Group 1 (x) practices Task 1.

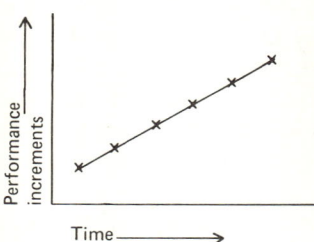

Learning of Task 2 by Group 1 (x) contrasted to task 2 learning by Group 2 (●). Effect, positive transfer, may be immediately apparent, as shown,

or

positive transfer effects may be seen in later stages of learning, as shown.

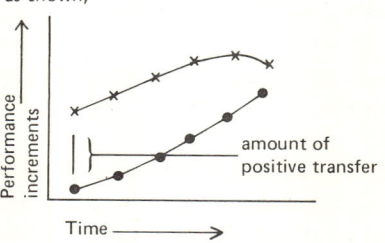
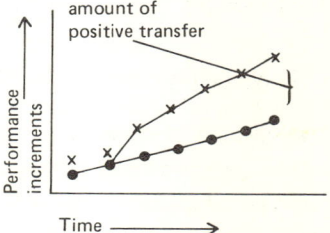

Figure 8.2 *Evaluation of transfer effects.*

C. Retention, another measure of transfer

Occasionally, immediate performance changes do not occur, but previous practice of one task influences retention of a second task, after a period of no practice.

Group 1 (x) practices Task 1.

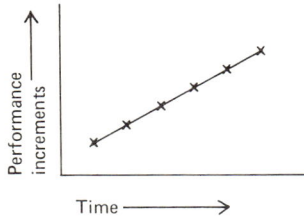

Performance measures are obtained on Task 2, with no difference recorded between Group 1 (x) and Group 2 (●) in effort.

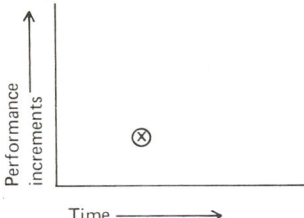

Retention measures may, however, reveal intergroup differences in performance of Task 2.

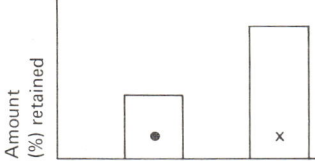

D. Transfer, and specifically retention effects, may be studied by comparing effects of a practice task on a previously practiced skill (**retroactive facilitation or inhibition**), or by comparing effects of a practice task upon another task practiced after the initial task (**proactive facilitation or inhibition**). **Retroactive** effects may be studied within the following context:

Groups	Initial task	Task interpolated	Recall
Experimental group	Practices Task 1	Practices Task 2	Task 1
Control group	Practices Task 1	Rests	Task 1

Proactive effects may be studied within this context:

Groups	Prior practice	Desired task	Recall
Experimental group	Task 2	Task 1	Task 1
Control group	Rests	Task 1	Task 1

Figure 8.2 (*continued*)

4. The mechanics of a movement may be emphasized when one practices with the nonpreferred hand, necessitating careful thought about how the total body supports the movement.
5. When learning new skills, students should not be taught bilateral transfer games; the most productive practice of one-handed tasks will, of course, be done by the hand originally intended to carry out the task.

INTERTASK TRANSFER

Helpful directions have been offered regarding transfer effects between tasks. Often, positive transfer is encouraged by having subjects engage in various practice tasks.

One pertinent question concerns the closeness of two tasks and the degree to which negative and/or positive transfer is likely to occur when one of them is practiced. While it is obvious that practicing identical tasks will result in positive interaction effects, it is questionable how different one task can be from another and still elicit positive transfer effects, and at what degree of difference negative transfer effects will ensue.

In general, the guidelines on this topic are rather vague. Figure 8.3 is presented to illustrate that when "nearness" is only moderate, negative effects are likely to occur because of the potential confusion.

Negative and/or positive transfer effects between tasks are more easily understood when stimulus and response elements of the tasks are scrutinized. For example, it is more likely that negative transfer effects will occur between two tasks when the stimulus elements are identical and the response elements are dissimilar. For example, many people have difficulty changing their driving habits from a car with a clutch to one without a clutch, or vice versa. In both cases the stimulus conditions are highly similar—the view of the road, the appearance of the interior of the car, and so on—yet one situation requires precise foot–hand coordination to pair gearshift and foot pedal, while in the second, the foot is not as frequently involved in driving. Practice in a car with automatic transmission may inhibit performance in driving a car with a foot-operated clutch, and vice versa.

Similar analogies exist in athletics. Indeed, some common drills seem to violate the principle of similarity of both response and stimulus conditions. Basketball players, for example, often participate in a "tip-in" drill in which one player positions himself on one side of the basketball backboard and attempts to tip the ball back to the board and make it rebound to the other side, over the basket, to the second participant,

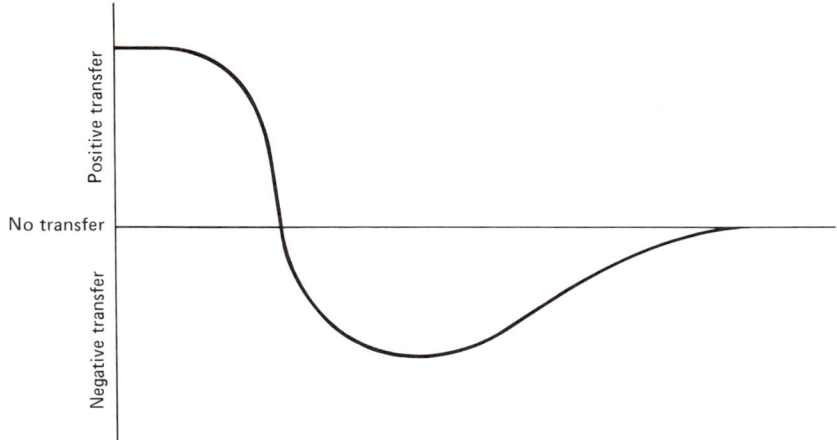

Figure 8.3 *Nearness of second task, and possible transfer to first task. If the second task is highly similar, positive transfer will usually occur. If the second task is not similar, particularly if the response elements are different, negative transfer may occur. If the second task bears no resemblance to the first task, no transfer will occur.*

who jumps up and attempts to duplicate the action in the other direction. Such a drill is supposedly preparatory for the game situation in which the task is usually to tip a rebound into the basket, scoring a goal. A strong case, however, could be made that the practice conditions are likely to produce negative transfer to the game situation, in which the response required is different, (tipping the ball *into*, not *over* the basket, as practice) while the stimulus condition (the ball rebounding from the backboard) remain the same from practice to game conditions. If, in practice, the participants practice tipping the ball *into* the basket, retrieving it, and repeating the action, it is more likely that positive transfer to the game situation will occur.

Negative transfer is less likely to occur, on the other hand, when stimulus conditions vary while the response remains the same. Extended practice by baseball shortstops, for example, in all the possible combinations of stimulus situations which would trigger a throw to first base or to second base, is likely to produce beneficial results. The throws remain the same from practice to game, while the stimulus conditions vary; but if the possible stimulus conditions (high bounder, low grounder, and so on) are anticipated, positive transfer effects are likely.

Of course, if the stimulus elements and response elements of two different tasks are obviously dissimilar, little negative or positive transfer between the two is likely; if stimulus and response elements are virtually identical, marked positive transfer effects will usually occur.

It is interesting and important to note, however, that if two tasks seem on the surface to be highly similar, and if learners are informed that they are similar, if real differences, even though slight, exist between the two, negative transfer effects may occur. A student of mine designed a study in which a group of junior high school students first practiced an underhand softball pitch for accuracy and then attempted to perform an underhand volleyball serve. Her assumption was that positive transfer would occur between the tasks, and she attempted to enhance these effects by informing her subjects that the two tasks were highly similar. She was somewhat chagrined, however, to find that negative transfer seemed to occur. Practicing the softball pitch produced less capable performance in the volleyball serve, than was recorded by a group with no prior practice in the softball pitch.

Closer analysis of the two tasks, however, revealed possible reasons for the negative transfer. The softball throw, of course, employs a heavier and smaller ball which rests in the hand during its swing backward and forward, while the volleyball, a lighter and larger missile, must be struck, and may be aimed differently from the softball pitch. Thus, though the arm seems to be traveling through the same arc in both tasks, and balls are involved, there are real although subtle differences between the two skills. However, if the learners became convinced, even though spuriously, of their similarity, they may have attempted to apply the same forces, velocities, and principles to both, and the resultant confusion could have caused the impediment in the second skill they attempted.

Another study, published in the 1950s, found no positive transfer between a task involving the use of a tennis racket and one in which a badminton racket was employed. The subtle differences between the two techniques—between badminton, in which wrist movement was more apparent, and tennis, in which wrist movement was minimized—perhaps caused the lack of transfer noted in the data.

Learning Sets

Research in the late 1940s opened another important door to the study of transfer of learning. Data suggested that not only do we learn in specific ways the various discrete stimulus and response elements of a given task, but also we probably learn how to learn groups of tasks within more general categories. In other words, with experience it is likely that we become more intelligent in our approach to and organization for various tasks within categories to which we have had previous exposure.

With practice, young children soon learn how to engage in tasks which require that they sort various kinds of objects, shapes, or pictures.[1] With increased experience at various agility drills, as a boy grows up and participates in athletics, he becomes more adroit at learning new agility drills, even though the response elements in the new drills may not be similar to the elements in familiar tasks. In other words, we learn how to learn; we become better at anticipating difficulties, at assessing our capabilities in relationship to the task, and at comparing the elements in new tasks to a reservoir of past experiences.

Thus, one must consider various generalized experiences, strategies, and feelings which may elicit positive transfer from task to task, in addition to the specific response elements within tasks familiar and unfamiliar to the learner. It would be expected that the following general qualities would elicit positive transfer between previous and subsequent motor tasks:

1. Positive feelings about participating in one physical performance may facilitate positive transfer to a second.
2. Learning how to analyze motor tasks, to break them down and to put them together, and learning the physical principles involved in physical performance, may encourage positive transfer.
3. Becoming aware of what cues are most important to an individual as he learns motor tasks (verbal cues, movement practice, visual demonstration)—in other words, acquiring self-awareness—is helpful when learning a motor task.

Positive and Negative Effects

It is often difficult to determine exactly why negative or positive transfer occurs between two tasks. In most situations some elements of the first task will exert negative effects on the second task, while some aspects of the initial task will facilitate performing and learning the second. The amount of negative or positive transfer depends on whether the negative outweighs the positive, or vice versa (see Figure 8.4).

Thus, if the maximum amount of positive transfer is to occur between two tasks, one should attempt to optimize the number of elements in the tasks, both general and specific, which will elicit positive transfer, and

---

[1] This generalized transfer effect between sorting tasks has been documented in retarded children.

116 TRANSFER OF SKILL

1. If negative factors outweigh positive factors, total effect is likely to be negative transfer.

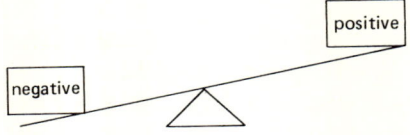

Negative transfer:
first task will cause second to be performed more poorly than if first had not been engaged in.

2. If negative factors are equal to positive factors, no transfer is likely to occur.

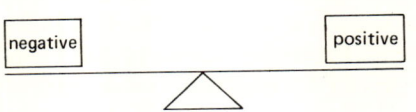

No transfer:
no positive or negative intertask influences occur.

3. If positive factors outweigh negative factors, positive transfer is likely to occur.

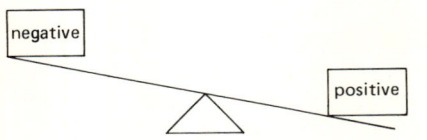

Positive transfer:
performance in first task will improve performance and/or learning of second.

Figure 8.4 *Relative influence of factors which might elicit negative or positive transfer effects, when two tasks are compared.*

to minimize those which produce negative transfer. Creating close correspondence of both stimulus and response elements, as well as attempting to elicit generalized transfer effects by pointing out the similar mechanical and intellectual elements in two tasks, is likely to accomplish the desired positive transfer from one to the other.

Many Transferable Elements

In addition to maximizing stimulus and response elements and generalized intellectual elements, one can produce positive transfer from drills to games by adhering to another important principle. To produce positive transfer from practice session context, to game, to final competition, one should attempt to expose the performer during practice periods to *many* transferable elements.

Coaches and instructors who concentrate exclusively on a single coordination exercise, or on one or two favorite drills, despite the resemblance of drill to final effort, may be less than productive.

Water polo coaches I observed recently were conducting drills which duplicated every possible way the rules allowed to carry a water polo ball across a pool. Many basketball coaches similarly conduct shuffle drills and other defensive exercises which duplicate the many possible ways players move their feet, body, and hands in defense. Coaches who do not conduct such comprehensive training programs are probably less effective than those who do. Athletes should not be asked to forget the effects of practice drills when confronted with game conditions. For example, a common drill for defensive linemen in football involves moving laterally across the field, rapidly crossing and uncrossing the feet. However, I have yet to observe this type of foot and body movement in the defensive backfield in actual playing circumstances. Instead of the foot-crossing drill, football coaches should carefully analyze the positions taken by the feet as defensive linemen move across the field, retreating backward to the left and right, rapidly changing position, moving forward, turning and running to the side, running forward to the left or the right. Drills should duplicate these movements precisely. At the same time care should be taken not to limit the number of drills, thus excluding some of the game movements from the drill movements. Coaches and physical education teachers who ignore this principle will probably be less effective than those who take it into consideration.

The quantitative relationship between the number of possible actions within the game situation and those incorporated in the drills is shown in Figure 8.5.

SUMMARY

Transfer of training refers to the possible influence of practicing and learning one task on the practice and execution of a second. These effects may be negative, positive, or not observable in the performance. Transfer can be studied by comparing performance in tasks executed by one person's various limbs, and by comparing intertask practice effects.

Maximum intertask transfer will occur to the extent to which the stimulus and response elements in the two tasks are identical, or when the response elements are highly similar, even though stimulus elements are different. Additionally, an ability to analyze motor tasks and the

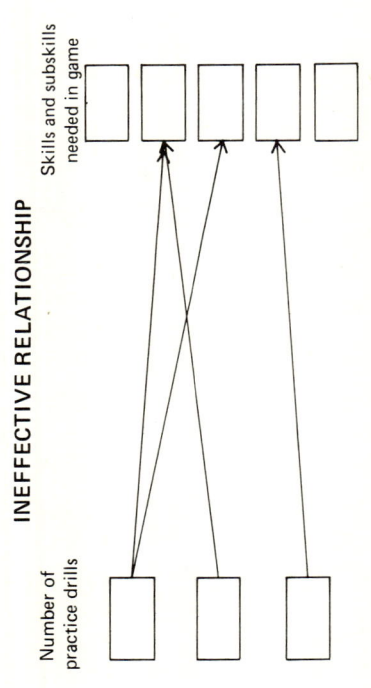
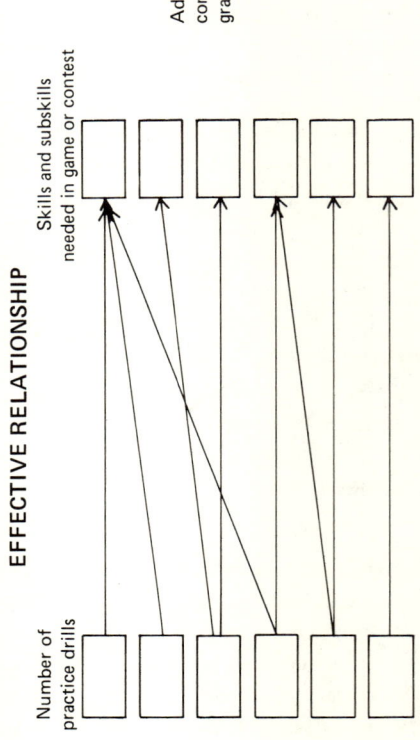

Figure 8.5 *Effective and ineffective drill-to-game-skill relationships.*

presence of similar intellectual elements in two or more tasks may facilitate positive transfer.

Maximum positive transfer effects will be elicited to the extent to which:

1. Drills are highly similar to the final performance.
2. "Intellectual bridges" of understanding are constructed by the instructor between the initial tasks practiced and the task to which it is hoped the practice effects will transfer.
3. Many transferable tasks are practiced, rather than only one or two, when a complex performance must be changed.

Negative transfer effects are minimized when:

1. An individual is not told that there are marked similarities between two tasks, when indeed the response elements are different.
2. The learner is helped to analyze carefully both the similarities and the differences in the numerous stimulus and response elements of the two tasks.

DISCUSSION QUESTIONS AND EXERCISES

1. If the final task is to field a ball hit directly to a shortstop and to throw it to first base, what practice tasks would be expected to elicit the maximum amount of positive transfer, maximum negative transfer, slight positive transfer, and slight negative transfer?
2. What does the concept of *learning sets* mean to an individual attempting to design drills for a football team?
3. How can the amount of positive transfer between two motor tasks be optimized? Be specific.
4. What is bilateral transfer? What practical implications might this phenomenon have?
5. How might intellectual and verbal components in skill be employed to elicit positive transfer?
6. How might a teacher or coach employ information about transfer of skill as he introduces a skill or sport to a class or team?
7. Design practice drills which will elicit maximum positive transfer to defensive movements in basketball. What should you do before designing the drills?
8. Design a drill which would elicit maximum positive transfer to shooting a jump-shot from the corner in a basketball game.
9. What general principle would you follow in designing a series of drills helpful to a goalie in soccer or water polo?

10. Can bilateral and intertask transfer be studied within the same experimental situation, using the same two tasks?
11. In what ways can transfer effects be measured?
12. What are retroactive and proactive facilitation and inhibition, with reference to sports skills? How do they affect weekday practice sessions, in relationship to weekend games?

BIBLIOGRAPHY

CRATTY, BRYANT J., "Transfer," Chapter 18 in *Movement Behavior and Motor Learning* (2nd ed.). Philadelphia: Lea & Febiger, 1967.

ELLIS, HENRY, *The Transfer of Learning*. New York: The Macmillan Company, 1965.

OXENDINE, JOSEPH B., "Transfer of Skill," Chapter 4 in *Psychology of Motor Learning*. New York: Appleton-Century-Crofts, 1968.

9

Retention of Motor Skill

Well-learned motor skills are usually retained for a relatively long period of time. One classic study, which sampled subjects' typewriting ability at twenty-five year intervals, revealed a remarkable amount of retention even though subjects did not practice during the intervals between tests. The same phenomenon is usually observed when skills employing larger muscle groups are practiced well and later reperformed after an interval during which no practice takes place.

The factors which influence the retention of motor skills have only begun to be researched, and at the present time there are no firm theoretical foundations on which to base an understanding of the manner in which motor skills are remembered. The practical guidelines and theoretical assumptions which are beginning to appear in the literature on the subject should help teachers to elicit better retention, and students to approach skill practice in ways which will lead to relatively permanent acquisition.

Scientific literature contains many more studies of how verbal material is learned, forgotten, or remembered, than of the same parameters of motor skills. Because many of the initial experiments required subjects to retain lists of nonsense syllables ("meev," "lerm," "jish," "crad," and so on), most of the findings cannot be used to construct valid principles about the retention of coherent written or verbal materials, and they are even less helpful in explaining the factors influencing motor skill retention.

For example, it was usually found that when nonsense syllables were learned reasonably well by the subjects and then represented to them after a period of no practice, marked forgetting began shortly after the first practice session (see Figure 9.1).

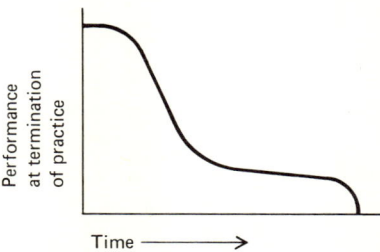

Figure 9.1

On the other hand, longitudinal studies of motor skill produce forgetting curves which, while revealing some immediate loss of proficiency, generally do not decline as fast as when the repractice involves nonsensical written and verbal material. Thus, the forgetting of many motor skills, plotted by connecting performance scores, would appear as in Figure 9.2.

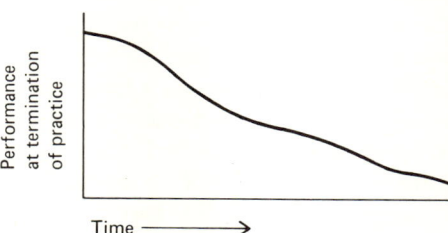

Figure 9.2

There are several reasons for the difference in retention of verbal and motor skills, even though most so-called motor skills are heavy with verbal, conceptual, and perceptual components. Thus, retention of some motor skills is governed more by laws covering the retention of verbal information, than is retention of other skills whose execution is not as heavily dependent on verbal mediation.

Understanding some of the theories explaining motor skill retention will allow better planning for retention, as will information on specific conditions which seem to heighten the ease with which a skill is re-performed after a period of no practice.

Theories of Retention

Two types of theories attempt to explain how humans remember both verbal and motor skills. One type, aptly termed "models," employs information from research into the neuroanatomical and biochemical underpinnings of learning and retention. A second category includes theories which are based on observation of behavior and events which seem to influence memory, retention, and forgetting. Most of our discussion will concern the second group of theories; the reader interested in neurologically- and biochemically-based theories of learning and retention should refer to the texts in the bibliography at the end of this chapter.

The earliest theories of how humans remember or forget might be termed "decay" theories. Because an increased amount of forgetting occurred over time, it was suggested that memory traces decay, and that the duration of the interval between the termination of the initial practice and later reperformance was the most influential factor in forgetting and remembering. As we have seen, however, much of the early research involved lists of basically meaningless nonsense syllables; subjects evidenced marked and rapid memory loss because they had no reason to remember the nonsense lists.[1] Since the early decades of this century, however, more elaborate research studies have disclosed that several other interacting events seem to mold memory, retention, and forgetting, in addition to the time during which an individual is expected to remember information. Thus, later writers have proposed that most important to retentional processes are the quantity, nature, and quality of various events which may interfere with the memory process (see Figure 9.3). Interfering events may occur before the task to be remembered, or between the initial practice and the retest of the reference skill.

The interpolated events can prove helpful to retention, particularly if

---

[1] A case could be made that intellectual behavior includes the ability to forget quickly meaningless material, events, verbiage, and the like. Retardates, for example, often retain meaningless information, for example, all the flight numbers at the airport they have visited a week before, indicating that a breakdown in "selective forgetting" is often a sign of less than adequate intelligence.

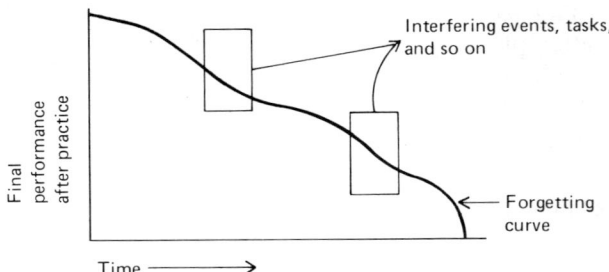

Figure 9.3

they are highly similar or in other ways make the skill which is later tested for retention more vivid. In other cases the events can prove disruptive to retention of the skill to be reperformed. For example, a great deal of verbal material bearing only a passing resemblance to verbal information which is to be retained may interfere with the memory of verbal skills. Indeed, some have suggested that the primary reason verbal information seems more difficult to retain than motor skill is the great amount of verbal information to which people are exposed daily. This information causes interference in the retention of verbal material, whereas daily confrontations with highly similar motor skills are not so frequent.

The most viable theoretical explanations of why we remember and forget motor skills to varying degrees incorporate the concept of decay over time as well as that of the influence of interfering and facilitating events during the period of no practice. That is, the degree to which we remember or forget how to execute a motor skill depends on both the length of time during which no practice has occurred and the nature of events similar to, different from, and possibly emotionally disruptive and/or physically taxing which occur while no practice has been engaged in and before the retesting of the skill itself.

While some researchers assume that motor skills are more resistant to forgetting than are verbal skills or written material, a comparison of the difficulty of the two types of skills (verbal and motor) is needed to support their statements. It is difficult to determine whether one or the other type of skill is more easily retained because it is easier or is to some degree either verbal or motor. When such comparisons are made, with an attempt to keep the difficulty of the two types of skill the same, retention is found to be about equal. For example, one researcher exposed his subjects to two types of mazes (one a "verbal maze," the second a two-choice maze), executed by following with a finger the pathways of a raised wire, while blindfolded. Figure 9.4 shows the general types of mazes involved in the study. The study found that when

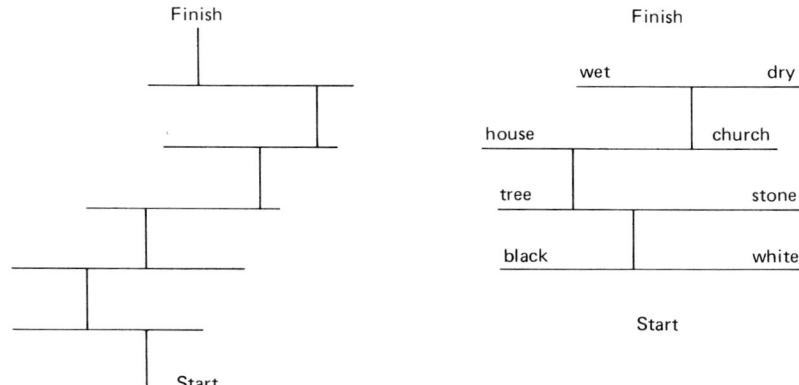

Figure 9.4 *(Left) Finger maze of raised wires, learned blindfolded. (Right) Subject is given first two words, guesses which one is arbitrarily termed "correct." When he does, he is given next two and again guesses which is "correct." When he does, he is given third set of two words, and in this way proceeds through the two-choice verbal maze.*

the difficulty of the motor and verbal tasks was equated in this manner, retention was about equal.

A thorough consideration of the retention of motor and verbal skills indicates that some verbal skills and written information are as easily retained as are rhythmic movement tasks. A simple childhood rhyme, for example, is as easily recallable as the skill of riding a bicycle, learned about the same time. A less rhythmic motor skill composed of relatively discrete elements is as difficult to remember as is prose, while complex movements which have little internal coherence (for example, move the handle to slot ten when a red light shows and to slot six when a blue light shows) are as difficult to retain as are lists of nonsense syllables. These comparisons are summarized in Table 9.1.

Table 9.1

	Motor Skills	*Verbal Skills*
Easy to retain	Rhythmic movements valued by the culture, such as swimming, bicycle riding	Poetry
Moderately hard to retain	Complex serial tasks resembling sports skills	Fiction, prose
Difficult to retain	Discrete responses to specific stimuli, having no rational relationship to each other	Lists of nonsense syllables

The Measurement of Retention

Retention has been measured in several ways. Although the reader is probably not about to embark upon research into that topic, it is important to outline briefly how the retention is objectively assessed.

One obvious way is to practice a skill for a given number of trials or until a given proficiency is reached, then to interpolate a period of no physical practice, and then to determine what percentage of the original skill level is evidenced during the retesting period.[2] This is called the percent-of-improvement method.

A second way is to begin with a period of practice trials usually leading to improved performance, then to follow with a period of no practice to determine how much time or how many trials are needed during the retesting period before the initial level of performance is elicited. This is called the savings method. Both methods are diagrammed in Figure 9.5.

Other, sometimes surprising things may occur when retention is evaluated. In a few cases, for example, during the period of no practice, some kind of spontaneous improvement seems to take place, and better performance is elicited after the no-practice period than at the final stages of initial practice! The possible reasons for this "reminiscence effect" will be discussed later in relation to the influence of massed and distributed practice on learning and performance.

Short-Term Retention of Motor Skills

Relatively little information is available on the short-term retention of motor responses, as the primary intent of researchers is usually to evoke long-term retention of motor skills. The information which is available indicates that unless it is frequently practiced, a simple response will be quickly forgotten within a few seconds (for example, manually placing a slide a given distance down a straight track). Whether such short-term retention effects are due to prior interference of similar responses or to a time delay is difficult to determine; however, authorities indicate that this type of quick initial forgetting is attributable primarily to the time during which no physical practice takes place.

It is probable that short-term memory would be improved, and possible that the movement would drop into the long-term memory store of the individual, if mental rehearsal of the movement or skill took place immediately after the first practice. However, mental rehearsal of simple

---

[2] It is, of course, difficult to prevent subjects from engaging in mental rehearsal of a skill during the period of no physical practice, and they may persist in doing so even if asked to desist.

PERCENT OF IMPROVEMENT METHOD

Initial learning of ten basketball free throws without a miss, extending over ten practices of ten trials each, one practice a day.

One-week period of no practice

Retest indicates subject can perform seven free throws out of ten without a miss (70% retention)

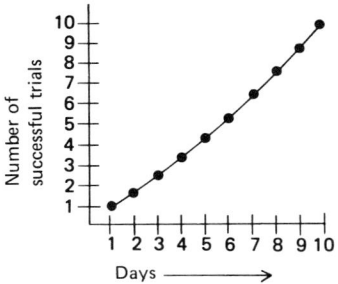
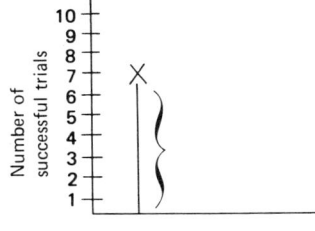

SAVINGS METHOD

Initial learning to proficiency (ten free throws without a miss) required ten practices, extending over ten days, with ten trials per day.

One-week period of no practice

On retest, subject initially performed seven free throws without a miss, then took four days, ten trials per day, to reach initial level of learning achieved (ten out of ten). This was a "savings" of six days, as contrasted to first learning sessions, or 60%.

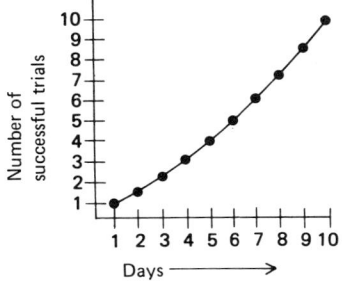
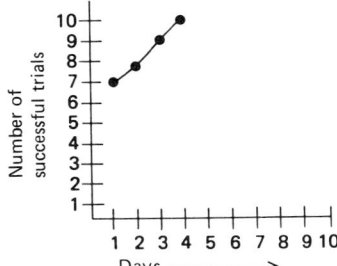

Figure 9.5 *The measurement of retention.*

motor skills is often difficult, particularly if the individual attempts to describe the movement verbally; some movements are simply not amenable to verbal translation. However, data on this and other important questions concerning short-term retention are rare at the present time.

Concern about short-term retention of motor skills and the auditory information accompanying motor skill practice is shared by most coaches and physical educators. The influence of short-term retention of the "feel" of a previous movement on its reperformance or modification is a potentially important factor in the final skill level achieved, as an individual experiments with different modifications of a reasonably complex task during the learning trials. Defects in the short-term memory of motor acts probably result in the inability to transfer the experience of one trial of a task to subsequent trials. However, until more is learned about this aspect of motor skill retention, it is difficult to validate guidelines for the coach and physical educator. For additional discussion of short-term motor skill learning, see Chapter 4.

Long-Term Retention of Continuous Responses

Relatively rhythmic continuous responses are probably more easily retained than are skills composed of many discrete elements. However, here again the available information is extremely limited.[3] One experiment, whose findings are typical of several carried out during the past sixty years, found that even after a twenty-four month period, a reasonably complex two-handed manipulative task coupled with the necessity to predict the movement of a visual display was performed at its original level of proficiency within a minute or so after its representation to the subjects.

Remarkable retention of continuous motor skills may be caused partly by the fact that fluid movements reinforce the performer constantly as they are executed, unlike the less frequent reinforcement (relative to knowledge of success) that occurs when verbal skills are practiced. Moreover, the unstructured motor skills performed daily may offer less interference with the more highly organized and coherent skills employed in laboratory experiments on long-term retention. It may be true that kinesthetic or movement stimuli are more amenable to being reinstated within the organism's response mechanism than are verbal information and discrete motor responses. All these suggestions, however, are only unsubstantiated assumptions until more evidence is available.

Long-Term Retention of Discrete Responses

Retention of discrete motor responses combined in various tasks is found to be like retention of verbal skills. In contrast to retention of continuous motor responses, studies of discrete responses find relatively rapid initial forgetting followed by almost complete forgetting within six months to a year. Not only are discrete responses more heavily laden

[3] In the late 1950s and 1960s some research on this topic was inspired by the need to study the retention of skills needed to land spaceships after prolonged trips.

with verbal components, but they are probably more behaviorally complex than the more fluid movement patterns. It is also probable that relatively high levels of initial learning are more quickly achieved in the more integrated fluid tasks than in tasks in which discrete, unrelated response patterns are incorporated.

An Overview

Both continuous and discrete responses are often called for in various sports. For example, basketball calls for smooth-flowing, rhythmic dribbling and shooting skills, which are not usually forgotten once they are well learned. Structured offenses containing a number of discrete responses, to be performed while the smooth-flowing skills are also called for, are more likely to be quickly forgotten upon the termination of competition or at the end of the season.

The same is true of other sports. In baseball, for example, the discrete moves which must be made in response to various situations on the field (runners on various bases with a given number of outs, for example) are difficult to learn and easily forgotten by the inexperienced as well as the experienced player. On the other hand, the rather fluid fielding, pitching, catching, and throwing responses stay with an individual until the physical mechanisms supporting them begin to deteriorate in middle age.

Thus, it seems that certain types of sports response patterns need more attention than others. For a discussion of the teaching characteristics and conditions dictated by the available information on motor skill retention, refer to Chapter 4.

Aiding Retention of Skill

Several valid guidelines should facilitate the retention of motor skills. Of overriding importance, for example, is the level of learning achieved before the period of no practice. The higher the level reached, the greater the retention; overlearning elicits retention.

However, there are limits of initial learning which, if exceeded, probably do not result in much extra retention. That is, the time needed to overlearn a task to a marked degree will not always translate into a similar amount of retention overtime.

For example, if the criterion task to be learned is making ten free throws in basketball of a possible ten attempts, learning the task to 100 percent of the criterion would mean practicing until ten of ten are executed without a miss. At this point overlearning could be carried out in at least two ways. An individual could practice until he made more than one set of ten perfect throws, or until he made twelve of twelve or fifteen of fifteen. In the case of one who made fifteen of fifteen, the criterion was exceeded by 50 percent; 150 percent overlearning had taken place.

Obviously, to exceed the criterion of ten of ten free throws would take more of the performer's and the coach's time. How much more would depend on the patience of both coach and performer, on the other demands on each of them, and on a number of other conditions. In any case, it should be asked how much extra time is worth the increased amount of retention which is likely to be evidenced if ten free throws are attempted after a time without practice.

Studies of fine and gross motor skill retention as a function of overlearning indicate that overlearning to about 150 percent of the criterion is most productive of best retention; practice over this criterion, for example, to 200 percent of the criterion, is not likely to produce proportional additional retention. What is most difficult to determine in motor tasks not as easily measurable as making or missing free throws is what is a perfect or better than perfect performance. Thus, the exact guideline we have used is primarily applicable to motor tasks whose performance success may also be as precisely measured.

As we have seen, a second factor influencing retention is the integrated and fluid nature of the task. While the basic nature of the task cannot always be manipulated by the instructor, he can help the learner perceive relationships between task components which may make the total response pattern more understandable to the learner, leading to greater retention because of the intellectual relationships perceived between task components.

A third factor is whether the learner is informed that he must reperform the task at a later date. When this information is given to individuals about to learn motor skills, they seem to attend to the tasks differently and to learn better, or at least more thoroughly. While it can be assumed that most mature learners are practicing for retention, this assumption cannot always be made of immature and/or retarded individuals. Even sophisticated learners should be made to see how and when the skill they are practicing relates to others and fits into the total game, and should know when they will be held responsible for the skill they are practicing. If these guidelines are followed it is likely that greater retention will occur than if they are omitted by the instructor or athletic coach.

There is slight evidence that other factors play a positive role in the retention of skills. For example, some researchers find that "serial position" has the same influence on the retention of movements, as it does on recall of verbal information. That is, those items (or movements) placed during the initial part and at the end of a series are more likely to be remembered than those in the intermediate portions of the series. Keeping this principle in mind, we might ask ourselves several questions while teaching:

1. What points do I wish to emphasize in my lesson each day, and within my lessons during the school year? How may I place them best for optimum retention?
2. Should I attempt to repractice and reemphasize skills or principles which may tend to "hide themselves" within the middle of the school year, or within daily lessons containing other skills and principles?

Theoretically, the serial order effect on retention is caused by (1) the fact that an increasing number of the initial parts of a series are remembered, until the learner cannot retain any more and his memory mechanism seems to break down, while (2) the final parts of the series are also remembered reasonably well, because the ending has a delineating effect and the learner can "remember back from the end" to some degree. But whatever the reasons, the difficulty of remembering the intermediate portions of a lesson and/or series of lessons, and the relative ease of remembering the initial and final portions, if taken into consideration during the planning of individual lessons and total curriculums, should make the content of physical education and athletic programs more likely to be retained and reperformed well.

The admittedly sparse literature does not indicate that *how* a skill is learned can make much difference in the degree to which it will be retained. That is, whether the skill has been practiced in sessions closely spaced over time or at infrequent intervals, or whether the task has been learned in parts or as a whole, is not apparently as important as the *level* of final performance achieved before the retention interval is inserted. While it is true that the speed with which the final level of learning-performance is achieved, before the insertion of the retention interval, is influenced in part by the nature of the practice schedule, the schedule itself does not seem to exert a marked influence on retention; at least, it is not so important as the level of performance achieved.

Other factors which are potentially influential on the retention of motor skills, have not been extensively confirmed. Researchers in the 1930s found that as an individual begins to learn a task and nears its completion, there seems to be a heightening of what they termed the performer's "need strain." Furthermore, it was found that if a lesson is discontinued before its completion, the parts learned are more likely to be retained than if it is practiced to completion, the termination occurring when the need strain has lessened.

While the influence of incompletion on retention of motor skills has not been extensively researched, it would seem that sometimes instructors should fail to supply all the answers to performers, keeping them in at least temporary suspense about the ways of performing a complex skill, and encouraging them to strain to understand the performance principles of motor skills to which they are exposed. In any case, the reader may wish to experiment with this principle when it seems appropriate in his teaching.

SUMMARY

Although there are few theoretical and practical guidelines governing motor skill retention, the current literature suggests the validity of the following principles for teachers and coaches:

1. Retention is positively affected by high initial levels of learning on the part of learners who are aware of the future implications of their initial practice.
2. Retention may be negatively influenced by similar or interfering motor skills practiced during the retention interval, or having been practiced before the reference skill.
3. Short-term retention of even simple motor skills seems remarkably poor. However, qualitative practice of continuous motor skills produces high levels of retention after prolonged periods of no practice.
4. Continuous rhythmic motor skills are more easily retained than are more complex skills composed of discrete and independent units. The latter are similar to difficult verbal skills in the degree to which they are retained.
5. How one learns a motor skill is not so important to retention as to what level the skill is initially learned.
6. The same serial position effects seen in verbal skills are present when a series of motor skills are learned and then reperformed after a period of no practice. The initial and final parts of the series are best remembered, but the intermediate portions of the series are poorly retained.
7. Retention is measured after varying periods of no practice by assessing the percentage of the initial skill which is redemonstrated and/or by determining how long or how many trials are needed to demonstrate the original level of performance.

DISCUSSION QUESTIONS AND EXERCISES

1. In what two ways can retention be measured?
2. How would you facilitate the maximum retention of motor skills?
3. What reasons might be given for the apparently better retention of motor skills versus verbal information?
4. What types of theories attempt to explain the retention and forgetting of motor skills and of verbal information?
5. What would you tell students who you hope will retain a given motor skill?
6. Which sports skills involve discrete responses, which involve continuous responses, and which involve a combination of continuous and discrete responses? Which of the above categories of skills are likely to be retained?
7. What effect does serial position have on skill acquisition and retention? What guidelines might you formulate when preparing curriculum and daily lessons, relative to serial position and retention of skill?
8. What kinds of mental and motor activities might be engaged in during the retention interval which will either heighten or reduce retention of the initial skill practiced?
9. How can short-term retention be changed into long-term retention of skill?

BIBLIOGRAPHY

ADAMS, JACK A., "Recall of Motor Responses," Chapter 8 in *Human Memory.* New York: McGraw-Hill Book Company, 1967.

BILODEAU, EDWARD A., "Retention," Chapter 7 in *Acquisition of Skill.* New York: Academic Press, Inc., 1966.

FITTS, PAUL M., "Perceptual-Motor Skill Learning," in Arthur W. Melton, ed., *Categories of Human Learning.* New York: Academic Press, Inc., 1964.

FITTS, PAUL M., and POSNER, M. I., "Human Capacities in Perceptual-Motor Skills," Chapter 6 in *Human Performance.* Belmont, Calif.: Brooks/Cole Publishing Co., 1967.

FLEISHMAN, EDWIN A., "Individual Differences and Motor Learning," Chapter 8 in Robert M. Gagné, ed., *Learning and Individual Differences.* Columbus, Ohio: Charles E. Merrill Publishing Co., 1967.

JOHN, E. ROY, *Mechanisms of Memory.* New York: Academic Press, Inc., 1967.

KNAPP, B., "Retention, Transfer of Training and Motivation," Chapter 6 in *Skill in Sport.* London: Routledge & Kegan Paul, 1963.

KONORSKI, JERZY, *Integrative Activity of the Brain.* Chicago: The University of Chicago Press, 1967.

Milner, Esther, *Human Neural and Behavioral Development.* Springfield, Ill.: Charles C Thomas, Publisher, 1967.

Norman, Donald A., *Memory and Attention: An Introduction to Human Information Processing.* New York: John Wiley & Sons, Inc., 1969.

Sage, George H., "Conditions Affecting Motor Skill Acquisition and Performance: Practice," Chapter 17 in *Introduction to Motor Behavior: A Neuropsychological Approach.* Reading, Mass.: Addison-Wesley Publishing Co., Inc., 1971.

10

Summary and Overview

Many situations in which motor skills are acquired can be as rewarding to the learner as they are to the teacher or coach. Much of this satisfaction stems from the joy of expanding one's movement capacities by acquiring new forms of motor experience. Individuals can learn motor skills quickly and efficiently when they feel happy and motivated.

Exposure to motor activity, however, is not always a happy and satisfying experience. The clumsy child is often ridiculed by his peers and sometimes even by those hired to instruct him in physical education. The coach may become verbally abusive with his team during halftime, perhaps venting personal frustrations which in turn reflect his ineptitude as a coach. The factory foreman may similarly berate his subordinates on the assembly line when they seem to have difficulty benefiting from his tutoring.

Principles presently resting on reasonably solid data may maximize the chances for motor skill learning to be carried out successfully and within a supportive emotional environment. Many of these guidelines have been spelled out earlier in this book; deeper insight into them and into other helpful principles and practices may be gained from the literature in the bibliographies at the end of each chapter.

Remember that the translation of principles to real-life situations depends on the insight and sensitivity of the reader. It would be utterly impossible even in a text many times the length of this one to describe comprehensively how one should apply oneself to each of the hundreds of thousands of situations met when attempting to tutor motor skills. Thus, the translation of the following principles into operational procedures must rest with the reader.

In general, however, the reader who operates from a sound base of research-oriented guidelines, rather than from rigid recipes for action, will be superior in several ways. A thorough grounding in basic valid concepts underlying the "whys" of learning and teaching will make one more flexible, able to accommodate to a wider variety of people situations than someone who is not as theoretically grounded. A thorough background in theory will also enable the teacher-coach to evaluate more adequately new ideas and practices. Finally, flexibility and scholarly insights, which should come from discovering basic principles as an undergraduate, should help a fledgling teacher-coach to accommodate better to individual differences in the children, youth, and adults he will encounter in his career. For these reasons, the main points of this text are summarized below.

Variety in Teaching Methods

Effective teachers and coaches are comfortable using a variety of teaching methods. They do not feel that "everyone must learn as I do." They realize that some people learn best by demonstration, others by being given chances to practice within the teaching regimen; they know that some may need a detailed verbal description of what is required.

It is apparent that certain methods work best at various stages of the learning process. What works during the initial stages of learning may not be as effective as another approach during the later stages. An effective teacher is ready to change from proven methods, when their effectiveness seems to diminish, to new methods; he does not habitually use and reuse favorite methods.

Give Learners Time

Data on the effects of spacing practice in time indicate that many learners cannot be rushed when attempting to acquire motor skills. If practice sessions or performance trials are relatively long, rest periods must be similarly prolonged.

Before the learner is told of his relative success, he must be allowed some time to interpret the feel of the act; then he can deal with the information.

Surprisingly, spontaneous skill acquisition was seen in several studies in which performers were permitted long rest periods, lasting days or even weeks, between trials. On the other hand, imposing severe time stress on skill acquisition often blocks performance and learning and reduces retention.

Be Cautious of Overteaching

Sometimes the best efforts of coaches and physical education teachers may confuse or otherwise interfere with skill acquisition. Too many instructions, given too rapidly, tend to overload the perceptual capacities of the learner. Studies carried out in England for the past twenty years, dealing with "channel capacity," indicate that an individual is usually able to attend to one type of information at a given time. Thus, the teacher's instructions may actually conflict and interfere with the instructions the performer is giving himself, and with the kinesthetic information he is attempting to decipher as he completes a task. A good question for the teacher to ask a relatively mature performer after a performance trial is "What did you think about that?" He should ask this rather than attempting to impose too soon his feelings and thoughts about the performance.

Involve the Learner Intellectually

It is important to assume that the learner, even if considered retarded, has some degree of intellectual ability. Not only may he be analyzing the task, relative to his background and competences, better than the teacher, but he may also be engaging in mental practice of various types before or between performance trials.

Less mature learners may have to be introduced to the concept of mentally rehearsing skills. Their attention may have to be directed to the task, even when they are not performing, by giving them information to use in conceptualizing the task in verbal or visual terms.

If the situation warrants, the learner may be given decisions within the learning process. When children and youths perceive the performance situation as at least in part "their own thing," they are likely to apply themselves more vigorously than if they are dictated to in too authoritarian a manner.

Transmit Reasons and Meanings of Movement

It is invalid to assume that individuals learning motor skills are unthinking automats who will perform when told to and will engage in drills because the coach feels them to be important. Greater positive transfer will occur if bridges of understanding are formed by the learner between the drill and the hoped-for outcome. Additional research indicates that as children become older they are less likely to perform well simply to receive verbal praise or to earn some kind of material reward such as lettermen's jackets, trophies, emblems, or special uniforms. As children mature they tend to look for meanings within the tasks confronting them. They may ask themselves, "Is mastery of the task worth the effort?" "What good will this skill do me when I finish school?" "How interesting is this performance?" "Is this situation complex enough to offer a challenge?"

Coaches and physical education teachers who do not somehow provide challenge and offer reasons better than "do it because it is always done" for accomplishing goals are likely to find themselves wondering why their students are not motivated, do not display more efforts, and seem to be resisting their curriculum content.

Emotional Aura Is Important

Teachers of physical skills who ignore the emotional environment in which they operate are likely to be less than effective. Sometimes the nature of the situation is difficult to control or to change. At other times the teacher or coach can directly influence the situation. His gestures and words and how he organizes individuals for competition all have either a positive or negative influence on children and youths attempting to improve in motor skills.

Skills are usually learned best if the emotional context in which they are practiced is relatively accommodating and encourages best efforts without overactivating the learners.

Make Drills Effective

The optimum use of drills depends on several factors: how closely they are related to the game or final performance situation for which they are designed, the extent to which the learner perceives relationships between the drill and the desired result, and the extent to which stressful perceptual conditions within the drill situation resemble those in the final performance in which improvement is desired.

For example, in baseball infield play, using baserunners during field drill practice better prepares the infielders to accommodate to the often confusing movement of baserunners and the approach of the ball in the actual game situation. Other examples of this include using defensive players while practicing field goal kicking and pass catching in football practice.

Quick Improvement Is Motivating

Teachers and coaches should teach as much of a given skill, or as many important game skills, as quickly as possible. It is motivating, particularly for less mature children, to acquire game or performance skills rapidly. Overanalysis can prove oppressive; breaking a skill into component parts is not necessarily helpful. If the learners are mature and the skills are relatively simple, each may be taught as a whole. Only when one or more students cannot acquire a skill should it be broken down into component parts, and then only for those who have not been able to deal with the entire task initially.

Too much lecturing and analysis accompanying skill learning is not helpful. Students in elementary and secondary school are not interested in what their teachers learned in undergraduate theory classes. They usually want to get on with practice. This assumption, however, does not excuse a coach or teacher from obtaining thorough preparation in all possible components of performance and athletic situations. One outstanding swimming coach has a penetrating interest in and knowledge about fluid hydraulics; however, he does not feel that a lecture on this topic is always helpful to his swimmers in training.

Retention Is Best When Skills Are Well Learned

Skills are retained best when they are initially well learned. There is no substitution for overlearning when it is desired that a skill be re-performed at a later date. However, other factors will also enhance retention. For example, if a skill is meaningful and important to the learner it will be retained, particularly if he has initially gained an awareness of where, when, and why he will be asked to repeat it.

Conclusion

The development of skill in children and youths requires sensitivity in teaching and accommodation to individual differences in value systems and in physical abilities. Skill is enhanced if the learner perceives the immediate and future meanings of the movement to himself. The most effective teachers and coaches are those who best pair their attempts to instruct with the performer's efforts to teach himself. The more capable teachers of motor skills are those who understand the most about the individual potentials of their students and who respect and best accommodate to their different capabilities.

Index

A

Ability traits, 21
Academic achievement, and fitness, 98
Academic performance, and fitness, 95
Activation, 81
   definition of, 88
   and performance, 89
   techniques to modify activation level, 89
Adams, Jack, 13, 133
Affiliation needs, 86
Ammons, Carol, 4
Ammons, Robert B., 4, 13, 80
Appley, M., 93
Arousal and activation, 89
Athletes
   aiding in adjustment of activation-arousal level, 90
   psychology of, 3
   and social rewards, 87
   tactical training of, 100
Athletic performance and memory, 102
Athletics
   intellectual demands of, 99
   social rewards of, 85

B

Balance, 31
Balancing activities, 17
Bayley, N., 3
Bechtoldt, H. P., 37
Beisser, A., 93
Bilateral transfer, 107, 108
   dimensions of, 111
Bilodeau, Edward A., 4, 13, 133
Bilodeau, Ina, 4, 13
Buxton, C. E., 14

C

Cattell, J. McKeen, 2, 13, 21, 37
Cattell, R. B., 25
Closed skill, 7
Cognitive-motor skill, 6
Competition, as a motive, 86
Compound tasks, 19
Connolly, K., 54
Continuous skill, 7
Coordination, 25
Correlation, definition of, 21

Cratty, Bryant J., 3, 14, 36, 37, 54, 68, 80, 93, 105, 120
Cumbee, F. X., 38

D

Decisions, transferring to the learner, 65
Definition
 of ability trait, 21
 of activation, 81, 88
 of correlation, 21
 of motivation, 81
 of motor educability, 48
 of motor skill, 5
 of teaching, 11
 of transfer of skill, 108
Demonstrations, and teaching, 61
Developmental dimensions of motivation, 82
Doll, Edgar A., 3, 14
Drills, and skill acquisition, 138
Duffy, E., 93

E

Ellis, Henry, 120
Emotional environment, and learning, 138
Endurance, strength, 30
Evaluation of transfer effects, 107, 109

F

Factor analysis, 23
Factor loadings, 23
Fine versus gross motor skills, 16
Fitness
 and academic achievement, 98
 and academic performance, 94
Fitts, Paul M., 38, 133
Fleishman, Edward A., 14, 24, 38, 133
Forgetting curves, 122
Functional psychology, 2

G

Galton, Francis, 2, 14, 21, 38
Gesell, A., 3

Griffith, Coleman, 3, 14
Gross versus fine motor skills, 16
Guilford, J. P., 105

H

Hall, Stanley, 2
Handwriting, 2
Harmon, H., 25, 38
Henry, Franklin, 4, 14
History of research, 2
 on motor skills in the U.S., 4
Hyperactive children, 99

I

Ideomotor training of athletes, 99
Inhibition, of skill and practice factors, 73
Instructions, 55
 dimensions of, 55
 emphasis on speed versus accuracy, 77
 interactions between instructor's and own, 59
 and the learner, 56
 and movement, 63
 philosophical implications of, 65
 and time, 57
 transferring decisions to the learner, 65
 verbal, 62
 videotape, 61
 and vision, 60
Intelligence
 and skill, 94
 and skill learning, 137
Intertask transfer, 112

J

Jacobson, E., 93
Jastrow, A., 2
John, E. R., 133

K

Knapp, B., 14, 54, 68, 80, 133

Konorski, Jerzy, 133

L

Lawther, J., 3, 14, 54, 80
Learning
 versus performance, 46
 and time, 137
Learning curves, 39
Learning sets, 108, 114
Lefford, A., 105
Lindquist, E. L., 14
Long-term retention of skill, 128

M

McCollom, I., 14
Manual abilities, 25, 33
Manual guidance, 64
Maslow, A. H., 93
Massing practice of skill, 70
Measurement
 of motor learning, 52
 of retention, 127
Memory, and physical
 performance, 102
Mental practice, 95
Merrill-Palmer Scale, 3
Meyer, M., 38
Minnesota Rate of Manipulation
 Test, 34
Motivation, 81
 affiliation needs as, 86
 and development, 82
 intrinsic to the task, 82
 measurement of, 87
 social, 85
Motor ability traits, 26
Motor development, and
 motor skill, 51
Motor educability, definition of, 48
Motor learning
 definition of, 39
 dimensions of, 40
 history of, in U.S., 3
 measurement of, 50
 research on, in U.S., 2
 theories of, 5

Motor performance, 15
 and memory, 102
 and mental practice, 96
 and rewards, 82
Motor skill
 definition of, 5
 and development, 51
 learning, intellectual
  components of, 95
 practice factors, 69
 qualitative aspects of, 69
 retention, verbal versus
  motor tasks, 125
 timing of practice of, 69
 transfer of, 106
 types of, 7
Motor versus verbal retention, 125
Movement speed, 32, 35

N

Needs, psychological versus
 physiological, 83
Noble, Claude, 54

O

Open skill, 7
Oseretsky Test of Motor Ability, 3
Overlearning, 129
Overteaching, 137
Oxendine, J. B., 54, 120

P

Part versus whole practice, 75
Pearson, Karl, 2, 21
Perceptual-motor skill, 5
Performance
 individual versus group
  performance curves, 43
 and rewards, 82
 transfer of, 106
 versus learning of motor skill, 46
Performance curves, 39
 individual versus group, 43
 types of, 44
Peterson, G., 38

Physical ability traits, 21
Physical fitness and academic work, 96
Physical performance
  and memory, 102
Physical practice versus mental
  practice, 96
Plateauing, of motor learning curve, 46
Posner, M., 38
Poulton, R., 7
Practice schedule, 70
  and performance levels, 72
Progressive-part practice, 75
Psychological needs, 83
Purdue Pegboard Test, 33

Q

Queletet, L., 2

R

Ragsdale, R. B., 3
Razzing, and motor performance, 86
Reaction time, 32
  complex, 35
Research, on motor learning, 2
Response time, 32, 35
Retention
  aiding, 129
  measuring, 127
  long-term, 128
  and overlearning, 130
  short-term, 128
  of skill, 121, 139
  theories of, 123
Rewards, and performance, 82
Rhythm, and motor skill retention, 125

S

Sage, G. H., 68, 80
Scale of Motor Development
  (Bayley), 3
Seashore, Robert H., 3, 14
Self-instructions, 56
Sensory-motor skill, definition of, 10
Serial-order effects on retention, 130

Short-term retention of skill, 127
Simple tasks, 19
Simpson, E., 38
Singer, Robert N., 54, 68, 80
Skill
  definition of, 6
  and distribution of practice, 70
  retention of, 121
Skill acquisition, 40
  and intelligence, 94, 137
  stages of, 48
Skill complexity, typology of, 18
Skill transfer, 106
  theories of, 111
Smith, K. U., 14
Smith, William, 14
Social motives, 85
Spacing practice, 74
Speed, 27
  versus accuracy, emphasis in
    motor skill instruction, 77
Staleness, of athletes, 46
Stanford-Binet, 3
Strength, dynamic, 25
Strength-endurance, 30

T

Tactical abilities, evaluation of
  athletes', 100, 101
Tactical training, of athletes, 100
Task complexity, typology of, 18
Teacher sensitivity,
  measurement of, 87
Teaching
  definitions of, 11
  methods, variety in, 137
  motor skills, principles of, 137
Temporal dimensions of
  instructions, 57
Theories
  of motor learning and skill, 5
  of motor skill retention, 123
  of skill transfer, 111
Three-level theory of
  motor behavior, 36

Transfer
   definition of, 106
   evaluation of, 107, 109
   intertask transfer, 113
   and learning sets, 108, 114
   positive versus negative, 115
   of skill, 106
   and skill elements, 117
   and stimulus-response elements, 107
   theories of, 111
Trumbull, R., 93

V

Vanek, Miroslav, 3, 105

Verbal instructions, 62
Verbal versus motor skill
   retention, 125
Videotape, use of, 61
Videotaped instructions, 61
Vision, and instructions, 60
Vocational therapy, 17

W

Whiting, H. T. A., 54, 68
Whole versus part practice, 75
Willig, L., 80
Wiseman, S., 105
Wundt, W., 2